D1544594

# THE HARLEM GLOBETROTTERS

AFRICAN-AMERICAN ACHIEVERS

# THE HARLEM GLOBETROTTERS

Josh Wilker

CHELSEA HOUSE PUBLISHERS
*Philadelphia*

**Chelsea House Publishers**
*Editorial Director* Richard Rennert
*Production Manager* Pamela Loos
*Art Director* Sara Davis
*Picture Editor* Judy Hasday

**Staff for THE HARLEM GLOBETROTTERS**
*Senior Editor* John Ziff
*Associate Editor* Therese DeAngelis
*Editorial Assistant* Kristine Brennan
*Designer* Takeshi Takahashi
*Picture Researcher* Alan Gottlieb
*Cover Design* Sara Davis
*Digital Photo Colorization* Robert Gerson

First Printing

1 3 5 7 9 8 6 4 2

Library of Congress Cataloging-in-Publication Data

Wilker, Josh.
The Harlem Globetrotters / Josh Wilker.

p. cm.—(African-American achievers)
Includes bibliographical references and index.

ISBN 0-7910-2585-3.
0-7910-2586-1 (pbk.)

1. Harlem Globetrotters. I. Title. II. Series.
GV885.52.N38W45 1996
323'64'097471—dc20          95-25515
                                 CIP

*Frontispiece:*
*The starting five for the 1951*
*Harlem Globetrotters. Left to right:*
*Ermer Robinson, Reece "Goose"*
*Tatum, Bill Brown, Bill "Pop"*
*Gates, and Marques Haynes.*

# CONTENTS

# AFRICAN-AMERICAN ACHIEVERS

# THE HARLEM GLOBETROTTERS

# 1

## "Let It Loose"

THE MINNEAPOLIS LAKERS tore teams apart. The National Basketball League (NBL) championship of 1948 was theirs. The 1948 World Tournament title was theirs. All season long, any team that had wanted a piece of the Lakers had limped away, defeated. But in late February 1948 the Harlem Globetrotters, who had not lost a single game all season, challenged the Minneapolis Lakers to a showdown in Chicago Stadium.

"There were mobs," said Lakers owner Sid Hartman, remembering the scene outside the stadium. "We had people waiting in line at 3:00 in the morning." By tip-off the arena was jammed as tight as a rush-hour subway. "You could not get into Chicago Stadium," Hartman declared.

As he took a long look around at the packed house, the Globetrotters' owner, a rotund impresario named Abe Saperstein, began to smile. For two decades Saperstein and his team had struggled just to stay in business. Now, more than 20 years after the team had played its first game in an ill-lit, nearly empty high school gym, big crowds were turning out to see the Harlem Globetrotters. A happy Saperstein put the team's history in a nutshell: "We played along with middling success until

*Minneapolis Lakers center George Mikan goes over the back of his Harlem Globetrotters counterpart, Nat "Sweetwater" Clifton, to grab a rebound in a contest between the two teams at Chicago Stadium. Globetrotter Babe Pressley sandwiches Mikan from the rear.*

1947," he said, "then—boingg!—we're famous."

The fans turned out to see the Globetrotter magic. They came to see Goose Tatum, "the Clown Prince of Basketball," coax a wild, hilarious circus from the middle of a basketball game. They came to see Marques Haynes dust opposing players with a jackhammer-fast dribble no one had ever even dreamed was possible. They came to see Babe Pressley, who could put so much backspin on a bounce pass that it leaped right back into his hands, and old Duke Cumberland, who had pioneered the kind of clowning that Tatum was making famous, and young Sweetwater Clifton, who, despite his hulking frame, could whip behind-the-back passes and zip up and down the court like a cheetah. Fans all over the country were eager to see the Globetrotters' amazing show. But on that night in 1948 at Chicago Stadium, the fans came simply to see if the Globetrotters could win.

Saperstein used his team's newfound fame to arrange the explosive clash with the Lakers. It was an irresistible matchup. Banned, as always, from the professional leagues, which employed only white players, the Globetrotters had traveled around the country in the 1947–48 season, seeking out opponents. They played nearly a game a night, 101 games in all, all of them on the road, against whomever would play them, from college all-star teams to small-town fives made up of aging gym teachers and overweight farmers. They arrived in Chicago to face the Lakers with a spotless 101-0 record.

But no out-of-shape plowboys or balding set-shot artists played for Minneapolis. The Lakers were a team for the ages. Their star, 6-foot 10-inch center George Mikan, was in the spirited early chapters of a career of dominance unparalleled in the history of professional basketball. In his eight full seasons in the pros, Mikan's teams would fail to

Renowned as perhaps the greatest dribbler in the game's history, Marques Haynes starred for the Globetrotters from 1946 to 1953. No less an authority than Earvin "Magic" Johnson, the greatest passer in the history of the NBA, would cite Haynes as his ballhandling inspiration.

win the league championship only once. The bespectacled giant, whose appearance called to mind an ungodly blend of a timid college professor and a huge slab of granite, simply overpowered entire teams of athletes determined to stop him. Yet he reserved a surprising, nimble-footed grace for the rare teams he could not simply scatter like so many piles of dried leaves. Whether by brute force or agile skill, Mikan got his points. He won the regular-season scoring title four times, and he topped all play-off scorers in all but one of his pro seasons. "Mikan was such a dominant force," said a rival, Fort Wayne Pistons forward Fred Schaus, "we were at a loss when it came to stopping him."

The 1947–48 edition of the Lakers, after racking up a 43-17 regular-season record in the NBL, had stormed to the league championship, dropping a

*Playing the high post, pivot-man Sweetwater Clifton prepares to hand off to a cutting Globetrotter teammate in this 1950 matchup with a collegiate all-star team. "Of the NBA's original blacks," wrote Nelson George of the 6'5" Clifton, who helped break that league's color barrier, "Clifton was the one with the kind of leaping ability and flair we now associate with the contemporary game."*

mere two games in their romp through the play-offs. As there was more than just one top professional league in those days, the Lakers were not satisfied that they had fully staked their claim as undisputed champions of the basketball world. They entered the World Tournament in Chicago—which gathered several of the best professional teams in the country—and continued their triumphant, season-long march. In the final game of the tournament, Mikan mightily rose to the challenge waged by a strong Harlem Renaissance (popularly known as the Rens) squad, pouring in 40 points to lead the Lakers to a 75-71 win.

The Laker win over the Rens struck an ominous note with the Globetrotters as they prepared for their meeting with Mikan's team. The Rens had long been the Globetrotters' chief rival as the best black team in the country. For the World Tournament they had bolstered an already strong team by getting Sweetwater Clifton on loan from the Globetrotters. But even Clifton could not help the Rens slow Mikan down. In that day and age, when basketball scores were relatively low, the news that one man scored 40 points in a single game against top competition hit like a blow to the gut.

Besides showcasing Mikan's awesome talents, the Laker win also revealed the astounding skills of Mikan's teammate, Hall of Fame forward Jim Pollard. Known as "the Kangaroo Kid," Pollard could leap high to block shots and snare rebounds from centers yet dribble and pass like a guard. Washington center Horace "Bones" McKinney attested to Pollard's above-the-rim style: "We used to know when Pollard had been in the building because the tops of the backboards would be clean where he raked them. You couldn't press him either. He was too good moving without the ball. He'd get by you in a cat lick."

Future Basketball Hall of Famer Slater Martin concurred. "Jim was one of the best you'll ever see," he said. Veteran guard Herm Schaefer, who had scored more points in the NBL play-offs than all but Mikan and Rochester Royal Hall of Fame guard Bob Davies, made the Lakers an even more complete team. Only one team remained for them to topple.

The Globetrotters took the floor against the Lakers on tired legs. They had played five games in the five nights leading up to the game in Chicago Stadium, a circumstance that won them no sympathy from the Lakers, whose long season's journey through the brutal NBL was marked with welts, bruises, and myriad scars. "You had to get killed to get a foul," reported one player. But the Lakers had learned to give more blows than they got. The menacing look in their eyes announced that they had learned that intimidation was one good way to grab a win. The game began, and bodies started flying.

Mikan led the Lakers to an early lead. The joy the Globetrotter team normally exuded, even when they were playing it straight and not for laughs, seemed to be missing, gone as surely as if it had been

*George Mikan drops in 2 of the 40 points he scored against the Harlem Renaissance team in the 1948 World Tournament in Chicago. At the time, 40 points was an unthinkable scoring total for an individual player in a single game.*

knocked loose by a crushing Mikan elbow to the ribs. Throughout the entire first half, the Globetrotters looked tired, tight, and at times even a little scared. At halftime, they staggered to their locker room, down 9 after having mustered only 23 points.

The Globetrotters emerged from their locker room for the second half determined to turn the game around. They started battling back. A year in the NBL may have taught the Lakers how to play tough, but the Globetrotters had learned how to fight during a 20-year struggle to stay alive.

For two decades, the Globetrotters had fought to overcome many obstacles. As black men in the first half of the century in America, they were often not allowed to eat in restaurants in towns where they had just played. Sometimes, after a game in a remote town, they had no place to sleep. They slept curled up in a car and ate cold sandwiches from a bag. But on the court, in game after game, challenge after challenge, the Globetrotters rose above the monstrous, institutionalized racial hatred that seemed to shape so much of their lives. "I never went out there with the idea of beating a team because they were white," said an early Globetrotter star named Inman Jackson.

"You can't play the game mad," Jackson continued. "At least I couldn't. I just wanted to beat a man in a game. If he was from a championship team, so much the better." Jackson knew that the struggle for excellence sometimes got rough. "Sure, we had our fights," he said. "But that was how the game was played."

Bob Gibson, a legendary pitcher for the St. Louis Cardinals, paid tribute to the early Globetrotters' defiant spirit. Before his Hall of Fame career in baseball, Gibson was a dominant basketball player for Creighton University. He earned a spot on a college all-star team that squared off against the Globetrotters. During the game, Gibson sparked a rally by knocking down four straight shots, all on acrobatic drives to the hoop. "This annoyed the Globetrotters extremely," Gibson said. "On one occasion, I drove the ball down the lane and flashed past one of their big men, Andy Johnson. The next time down, Johnson had a message for me. He delivered it with his elbow, which sent me sprawling, and included words to this effect: 'This is my territory, son. Come in here again, and it's your [butt].' "

Gibson came away from the confrontation with a painful bruise from the elbow and a sprained wrist from the fall. He also came away much wiser. Acknowledging the incident as "the best pitching advice I ever received," Gibson eventually made the Globetrotters' combative ways his own. During his career, Gibson backed away from no one. Slugger Reggie Smith summed up Gibson's career by saying, "The man was going to war when he pitched." He had learned from the Globetrotters.

The Globetrotters scratched and clawed their way back into the game against Mikan's team. They pressed the NBL champions all over the court, as if they had been glued to the Lakers' jerseys. No one had ever seen a team play defense like the Globetrotters played it. Tony Lavelli, a forward for the Boston Celtics, said that on defense "the Trotters are like a nest of bees buzzing in your face." Most teams in the late 1940s believed that the best defense was one in which every defender concentrated solely on his own man. The Globetrotters shunned this style to play an attacking, gambling, wholly team-oriented defense. Decades later, in the 1990s, a similar defensive style—infamously known throughout the league as "unleashing the Dobermans"—helped Michael Jordan and the Chicago Bulls win three straight National Basketball Association (NBA) championships.

On defense, as with many other aspects of the game, the Globetrotters were far ahead of their time. "They take chances and make defensive plays that would cause the average coach to tear his hair," said Lavelli. "When one player is taken out of a play, one of the others will switch over and cover the mistake. I've never seen a switch system as effective as that used by the Trotters."

In the second half, the Globetrotters also began to play their game on offense. Passes zinged around the perimeter, from player to player, then in to Tatum near the foul line, then back out again, the ball moving so fast it seemed to have a hummingbird heartbeat of its own. The Lakers suddenly appeared to be a step too slow. Haynes, dribbling at the top of the key, feinted so sweetly that his defender got tangled grabbing at ghosts and tumbled

*Jim Pollard of the Minneapolis Lakers takes it hard to the rack. With his athleticism and jumping ability, Pollard was in some ways the prototype of today's small forward.*

in a heap to the floor. Haynes darted toward the hoop, drawing Mikan to him, then dished to Tatum for an easy lay-in. The Globetrotters were starting to get loose.

"Ah, yeah!" called Tatum like a bandleader reveling in his band's fast, furious music. Fans who had never seen the Globetrotters were stunned by their game. The norm in professional basketball at the time was the turgid, grim style used by the Lakers, who liked to hold the ball until they could pound it in to Mikan inside. The Globetrotters shrugged this style off in the second half, running the floor, moving the ball, driving to the basket, and—not incidentally—smiling. The Globetrotters were having fun.

Duke Cumberland, a 13-year veteran of the Globetrotters, grabbed a pass in the high post, his back to the hoop. Mikan blocked Cumberland's path to the basket, looming, a bespectacled mountain of muscle. Cumberland decided to have some fun. Up to this point in the game the Globetrotters had not done any clowning. "They dropped their comedy against us," said Sid Hartman. "They wanted to win." It was generally thought that in a game like this, in order to win, the Trotters would have to stifle that part of their act. But the Globetrotters' greatness on the court derived in part from the fact that they did not stifle anything but let it all come tumbling out. Globetrotter veteran J. C. Gipson once explained the spontaneous approach of the team in his words to a rookie getting ready for his first game: "You feel something funny, let it loose."

Right there in the middle of one of the Globetrotters' biggest games ever, right there as George Mikan edged closer, readying to swipe and grab at the ball, Cumberland felt something funny. "Now you see it," he announced, holding the ball out at Mikan for a split second, then pulling it back, "and now, my friend, you don't!" Cumberland whipped the ball behind his back, around his waist, and between his legs, showing the befuddled Laker big man mere glimpses. Mikan swatted at what he glimpsed, but his motions, next to Cumberland's, made it seem as if his limbs were weighted down with lead. Cumberland capped his final magician-like flourish by stepping away from Mikan, the ball gone from his hands. The next moment lasted no longer than half a second, but it froze the world for everyone who was there to see what happened. The ball rested on Mikan's head. Mikan looked to Cumberland, in that half second unaware, and Cumberland, smiling, spread his hands wide. To add injury to hilarious insult, one of Cumberland's teammates grabbed the ball before Mikan could, wheeled toward the hoop, and laid in another Globetrotter basket.

Against most teams, such a play would likely signal the beginning of a rout. Mikan and the Lakers, however, still clung to a slim lead. As the game wound toward its conclusion, every stylish Globetrotter score, coming after several bullet-quick passes, would be matched by the brutish power of Mikan. "It was murder playing against Mikan," Bob Davies once said, speaking bluntly to match the blunt facts, "because when they needed two points he'd get the two points."

Throughout the history of basketball, the dominating big man has been hard to beat. The Globetrotters did not have a giant to counter Mikan on their team. Sweetwater Clifton was still smarting from the 40 points Mikan had dropped on him at the World Tournament, and Goose Tatum, dwarfed by Mikan, got into serious foul trouble simply trying to slow him down. But the Globetrotters kept up the pressure, playing their revolutionary game, a game built on ball movement, constant ball fakes, speed, and, as J. C. Gipson put it, the ability and will to "let it loose."

The Globetrotters played a new, exciting brand of ball built, in what seemed like a paradox, both on individual spontaneity and unmatched teamwork. Dutch Dehnert, a member of the team known as the Original Celtics that dominated basketball in the twenties and early thirties, was amazed by the

Globetrotter team of Tatum and Haynes. He claimed that the Trotters, as far as he was concerned, were the best team he had ever seen, noting, "The game was entirely different in my day, of course, but you'd have to give the nod to the Trotters for their speed and their fancy stuff. We had two basic plays—the give-and-go and the pivot. But the Trotters can feint you out of the building a dozen different ways."

Dehnert spoke for basketball's past. Another onlooker spoke for what was to come in the world of basketball after Tatum and Haynes and the rest were through working their joyous changes. "A two-hour workout with the Trotters," said a youthful coach of a West Coast college team, "is worth a full season of ordinary basketball training. You can't explain what makes them so unbeatable. You just marvel at them." The coach, John Wooden, studied the Globetrotters well. He went on to coach UCLA to 10 National Collegiate Athletic Association (NCAA) titles in 12 years, his team's fast, attacking, full-court style echoing the game the Globetrotters had pioneered.

In years to come, the Globetrotter style of play would influence basketball as it was played at its highest levels. The highly entertaining pro game of the 1990s has its roots in the way the Globetrotters of 1948 played when they were staking their claim as the best basketball team in the world. That team played with a disregard for the limits of what was previously thought possible. They spilled outside of the margins without losing control and so expanded the margins of what was possible. The future of basketball seemed to crackle and hum to life in the hands of the Harlem Globetrotters.

The ways of the past, epitomized by the Lakers' plodding style, would not give way so easily. With 90 seconds to go in the game, after the Globetrotters had finally grabbed the slimmest of leads, the

Lakers forced the ball down low to Mikan. Goose Tatum, bearing down on defense, got whistled for his fifth foul, which disqualified him. Mikan lumbered to the foul line and calmly knotted the score at 59 all.

Now the Harlem Globetrotters moved as one. The clock shed the final seconds as the players went into their figure-eight weave, a pattern of frenetic motion that the team carried off with a thrumming, otherworldly control. It was like a dance, and in its perfection it dimmed the importance of who won or lost the basketball game. A kind of joyous magic pulsed through the Globetrotters as passes winged fast from hand to hand. With three seconds left, the ball zipped to Globetrotter sharpshooter Ermer Robinson in the clear. Let it loose, Ermer Robinson. Let it loose he did: a perfect, graceful, high-arcing shot, the final buzzer blaring as the stung net jumped up laughing toward the sky.

# 2

## "Igloo and All"

THE TEAM THAT would come to be known as the Harlem Globetrotters started out as nothing more (and nothing less) than a good feeling. In 1926, some former players from an outstanding all-black Wendell Phillips High School basketball team in Chicago realized just how much they liked to play ball and win. They decided to try to keep that good feeling alive. Lester Johnson, Walter "Toots" Wright, Randolph Ramsey, Tommy Brookins, and Inman Jackson, all Wendell Phillips graduates, plus a former Wendell Phillips rival named William Watson, came together to form a semipro basketball team. Their manager, a black former football star named Dick Hudson, booked the team some games at Chicago's Savoy Ballroom, and the team had a name—the Savoy Big Five.

Basketball was far from being the main event at the Savoy. "The audience at the Savoy were people who wanted to be entertained," said one of the ballroom's most famous entertainers, singer and band-

*The 1930–31 Harlem Globetrotters five. Standing, from left, are coach and impresario Abe Saperstein, Walter "Toots" Wright, Byron Long, Inman Jackson, and William Oliver. Seated is Al "Runt" Pullins.*

leader Cab Calloway. "At halftime they'd roll this piano out in the middle of the crowd during the basketball game in the auditorium, and I'd start singing. I'd sing songs to the audience and by the end I'd have them all singing." For the Savoy Big Five, from the very beginning, the line between sports and entertainment was blurred. Like Cab Calloway, they were entertainers.

Unlike Cab Calloway, however, they were not very popular. The owners of the Savoy, seeing the sparse turnouts for the team's games, wanted to boot the Big Five out to make room for roller skaters. The team saw the writing on the wall and knew that to stay in operation they would have to start booking games elsewhere. This task proved easier said than done. Tommy Brookins claimed that Dick Hudson had trouble booking games because he was black. The fact that the team was not well known and that basketball itself was still a relatively new and unpopular sport certainly did not help the team's prospects.

To stay alive, the Big Five needed some kind of outside help. One day, Dick Hudson went out and got that help. He introduced to his team a 26-year-old youth league coach named Abe Saperstein.

What the team envisioned Saperstein's initial role to be is still debated. Tommy Brookins has stated that Saperstein was brought in at first merely because the color of his skin could help the team get more bookings. Saperstein always dismissed this interpretation, maintaining that he was brought in for his skills as a coach. The truth is probably some combination of the two stories. Not far removed from a successful high school basketball career, Saperstein undoubtedly had the ability to coach, and the color of his skin certainly could not have hurt in getting the team bookings. His burgeoning talents as a persuasive salesman and promoter would clearly have helped in this regard as well. Hustling

up games for the Savoy Big Five proved to be something Saperstein excelled at, almost as if he were
born to do it.

Abe Saperstein's story begins in Lomza, Poland.
It was there that his parents had gotten married,
planning to raise a large family. But Anna and
Louis Saperstein fled their native country to escape
the increasingly frequent pogroms (organized mas-
sacres of Jews). To greater and lesser degrees, anti-
Semitism would follow the immigrant family wher-

*The Original Celtics of New
York were one of the best
known of the early professional teams and carried on a legendary rivalry with the
Harlem Rens. Pictured here is
the 1923 Celtics five.*

*In the Roaring Twenties, bandleader Cab Calloway was a far bigger draw in Chicago's Savoy Ballroom than the Savoy Big Five, the basketball team that played there on Sunday afternoons and would ultimately become the Harlem Globetrotters.*

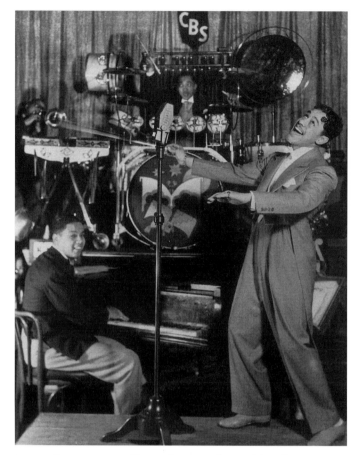

ever they went.  Years later, when Abe Saperstein was questioned about his ability to relate to the trials and tribulations of his black players, he replied, "My race also knew prejudice."

The Sapersteins moved first to London, where, in 1900, Abe was born.  Seven years later the family relocated to a poor, working-class neighborhood on the North Side of Chicago.  As one of the few Jewish children in a predominantly Irish and German neighborhood, Abe found out right away that he had to learn how to protect himself.  He learned how to fight by sneaking into a local gym where boxers trained.  Once he had won the respect of the other kids the hard way, Abe started making friends.  It was not long before the new kid on the block had become something of a neighborhood king. "Abe was a leader," his sister Fay once recalled. "He made friends easily and kept them. Our house was the headquarters for the boys in the neighborhood."

The large Saperstein clan often had to struggle to get by. Almost as soon as they were old enough to walk, the Saperstein kids had to work jobs when they got off from school. Abe remembered, "Some weeks we made as much as 25 cents apiece. We figured we were doing good. We didn't have much in those days, but we got along and we were happy."

Abe was never happier than when playing sports. Chief among his sporting pursuits was the relatively new game of basketball. The game that Abe played, which had been conjured up by a YMCA instructor named James Naismith only eight years before Saperstein's birth, was a far cry from the type of basketball that is played today. Its nebulous rules as to the number of players to a side and, more importantly, the amount of contact allowed, often made it resemble a war more than a sporting contest. An early coach named Marvin A. Riley told of one game from basketball's infancy in which two 40-man sides brawled to a scoreless tie. "If any one player did get his hands on the ball," Riley explained about the mutual shutout, "it took several minutes to dig him out from under the mob that immediately hopped him. I had 19 survivors and [the other coach had] 17, and on this basis we claimed the fight."

Though that game had occurred slightly before Saperstein's playing days, basketball still had a hard edge that made a kid from a poor, rough neighborhood feel at home. At that time, many games were literally played in cages, as a protective wire mesh separated the fans from the court. An early professional named Joel "Shikey" Gotthoffer recalled: "You could play tic-tac-toe on everybody after a game because the cage marked you up; sometimes you were bleeding and sometimes not. You were like a gladiator, and if you didn't get rid of the ball you could get killed."

Hoping to play college basketball, Abe Saperstein enrolled at the University of Illinois, but he had to drop out after one year for lack of funds. After leaving the university, he got a job working with neighborhood kids as both a counselor and a coach. "I get a big kick out of helping kids," Saperstein later reflected. "Maybe that sounds corny, but that's how it was."

Saperstein was still coaching the kids when Dick Hudson asked him to join the Savoy Big Five, an invitation akin to being asked aboard a sinking ship. The team's prospects at the Savoy Ballroom were growing worse all the time, and the team itself was on the verge of breaking up. Then three of the players, perhaps impressed by Saperstein's skills as a coach or as a promoter (or both), came to Saperstein with a plan, a scheme born, more than anything else, out of desperation.

"The night we made the decision," Saperstein remembered, "we had no definite plans. We just decided to bow out of the Savoy set up. There were three players—Walter 'Toots' Wright, Byron 'Fat' Long, and Willis 'Kid' Oliver—and me. The boys asked me to go along with them and I said yes. It didn't seem so at the time, but it was the best break I ever got. If we hadn't gone out on our own, I still might be hustling to make a living in Chicago."

Chicago may not have brought the team the success they wanted, but, after all, there was still a whole big country out there. Saperstein bluntly and boldly announced to a friend, "I'm going to put together a team and make money." The new team would differ a little from the Savoy Big Five. Saperstein bought a Model T Ford from the owner of a funeral home and told his team to get ready to hit the road. They were going to be barnstormers.

At that time, the only professional basketball leagues were small and generally short-lived. The best professional teams, by and large, barnstormed. It had been that way all through the early years of professional basketball. At the turn of the century, the New York Wanderers had roamed from game to game in horse-drawn carriages. A few years later, Basloe's Globetrotters, the brainchild of a fast-talking immigrant named Frank Basloe, replaced the Wanderers as the best barnstorming team in the land. By 1927, while Saperstein and his players packed their bags for their first road trip, Basloe's Globetrotters had faded. Still, it was a golden age for barnstorming basketball teams. A team of Chinese players called the Hong Wa Qs toured the Midwest while a Jewish team known as the Philadelphia

*In the barnstorming early days of professional basketball, the Globetrotters had to compete for the entertainment dollar with rival clubs such as the team representing the South Philadelphia Hebrew Association, which was usually referred to as the Sphas. The Original Celtics, the Harlem Renaissance, and the Sphas were generally regarded as the top professional teams during the Globetrotters' first years.*

*Clarence "Fat" Jenkins was a member of the original Harlem Renaissance squad of 1923 and continued to play with the team throughout the 1930s, when it was generally regarded as the finest basketball team in the country.*

Sphas (short for South Philadelphia Hebrew Association) traveled up and down the eastern seaboard. The House of David touring basketball squad took the court wearing fake beards. They were often confused with a team that shamelessly stole the gimmick and called themselves the Bearded Beauties. One of the most popular barnstorming teams, Olson's Terrible Swedes, featured the crowd-pleasing antics of Ole Olson, who thrilled and amazed with his behind-the-back passes. Gimmickry and flashy ballhandling had its place in barnstorming basketball in the late 1920s, but the two teams that stood out from all the others in this era—the Original Celtics and the all-black Harlem Renaissance team —played straight, no-frills basketball.

In that day and age—long before television and even before, in many places, the movies—the barnstorming teams brought an air of the exotic to the places where they played. Many of the people who came to see them had never ventured far from their hometowns and hungered to see a little of the world beyond their horizons.

Abe Saperstein banked on this particular kind of small-town yearning. One night, in his father's tailor shop, he stitched a new name into his team's uniforms: "Saperstein's New York." New York City, for the denizens of the small towns of the Midwest that Saperstein was hoping to lure, had the sparkle of the exotic. Saperstein was also perhaps trying to capitalize on the success of the one well-known black team of the day, the Rens, who hailed from New York. He would gradually hone his sense of what the public wanted, changing the team name to Saperstein's Harlem New York, then to the Harlem Globetrotters. " 'Harlem,' " he explained, "because I wanted people to know the team was Negro, and 'Globetrotters' because I wanted people to think we'd been around."

Andy Washington and Bill Tupelo joined Wright, Long, Oliver, and Saperstein. For the debut of the team that would soon be known as the Harlem Globetrotters, the six men piled into the Model T that had belonged to a funeral home owner and drove 50 miles west to Hinckley, Illinois. They won the game and got paid $75, each player receiving about $10, and Saperstein, as coach, business manager, and chauffeur, pocketing $20. The rest went to business expenses.

This seemingly humble start, as the team soon found out, would be one of the more lucrative of their earliest engagements. "When I started out with the Globetrotters," Saperstein later recalled, "my only aim was to make a fast buck. For a long time it was a very slow buck."

At a game in Chicago at the Loyola University gym, the fans barely outnumbered the players. A mere 27 people showed up to watch the game. Afterward, the owner of the gym, holding the $9.75 he had collected in ticket money, bluntly told Saperstein, "I don't know what I'm going to pay you with." Saperstein, erasing a pregame payment agreement with a shrug, replied, "Give me five bucks. We'll go out and get some sandwiches."

Though it too often happened in that first year that the best Saperstein could do was keep his players fed, he remained upbeat. He was, despite his words to the contrary, looking for more than just a simple fast buck. A desire for booming, overwhelming success drove him. He envisioned for his barnstorming team a fame so far-reaching that it would dwarf the popular acclaim of all the other traveling hoop squads. Years later, after the dream had finally come true, Saperstein proclaimed, "For years I dreamed of the time when we would be able to travel around the world, playing basketball as we went, and in places where it had never been played before." Saperstein had a motto that he would repeat to his players and to promoters and even to himself after games in depressingly empty gymnasiums. Keeping an eye on the future, he would say, "Maybe we'll be back through some time and things will be better."

It was not easy for the players to share Saperstein's belief that things would get better. For one thing, they were each paid half of what Saperstein received for every game. And some of the time that did not amount to much, certainly not enough to plan an entire future around.

Also, Saperstein did not have to endure the racially motivated indignities his players did. In those first short trips outside Chicago, the black players found themselves banned from all-white hotels and all-white restaurants. Worse, in some of the more remote places they traveled to, they were treated like monstrous exhibits in a freak show. A player named Bernie Price, who joined the team not long after its inception, described this dehumanizing phenomenon: "In some small towns the kids had never seen blacks before and they would rub our skins to see if the black would rub off. We were treated poorly practically everywhere."

Trying to stay alive, the struggling Harlem Globetrotters barely had a pulse at the end of their first season. The problems of a lack of funds and a lack of fans were compounded by the resignation of the team's lanky, athletic center, Andy Washington. A proud graduate of all-black Howard University, Washington could no longer bear the racial degradations the Trotters had to face on a daily basis.

For the other players, the desire to play ball outweighed the negatives. Also, Saperstein's persuasive and unflappable optimism proved contagious. A friend of Saperstein's, Philadelphia sports announcer Dave Zinkoff, once said, "Saperstein is a man of such persuasive charm that he could talk an Eskimo into moving to the Congo, igloo and all."

Saperstein knew all too well that in those early years, as he put it, "the possibility that the team would some day justify the 'Globetrotter' part of its title seemed as remote as a far-distant planet." He cast this potentially demoralizing likelihood aside and, in a feat only slightly less improbable than the one mentioned by Zinkoff, talked his players into believing that the Harlem Globetrotters had a future.

# 3

## "We Drove All Night"

INMAN JACKSON, A Wendell Phillips High School graduate and brief member of the Savoy Big Five, took Andy Washington's place on the team. The Globetrotters knew Inman Jackson could play, and it was not long before others were also singing the praises of the newest Harlem Globetrotter. The sturdy 6-foot 3-inch pivot man could rebound and block shots and zip bullet passes to teammates cutting to the basket. If the team needed a score, he could dizzy his defender with a couple of perfect ball fakes and waltz through the wide-open lane for a hoop. A former Notre Dame All-American named Moose Krause, recalling his many battles with the canny Globetrotter center, declared, "Inman was one of the greatest players in the game."

Jackson starred as the second-year barnstormers roamed and romped, conquering small-town teams throughout Illinois, Michigan, and Ohio. The team began to occasionally goof around before each game with a routine that showed off their ballhandling skills. Jackson, in particular, turned heads by rolling the ball down his arm and across his shoulder to his other arm. Though these pregame shenanigans would, over many years, develop into the Globetrotters' trademark Magic Circle, they were at this

*As the first center for the Globetrotters, Inman Jackson inaugurated the team's tradition of clowning at that position. One of the few ground rules the Globetrotters ever laid down for their opponents was that they were to be allowed uncontested passes into the high post, where most of the team's comedic routines, or "reems," began.*

early stage still a far cry from that later, finely polished act. According to Sidney Goldberg, a sports promoter, "When I booked them into Toledo for the first time in 1931—and gave them $43—the Circle wasn't that good."

After the opening tap, the clowning stopped. It had not yet occurred to the team to bring gags into the game itself. They concerned themselves with winning, and now, more than ever, they had the team to do it. Besides Jackson, the Globetrotters also added a fast, sweet-shooting guard named Al "Runt" Pullins. Sweetwater Clifton, who as a child growing up in Chicago in the 1930s got a chance to watch the team he would later join, viewed Runt Pullins as the prototypical Globetrotter for his transcendent basketball skills. On the hoop court, Pullins made his own rules. "He could do everything," Clifton said, "and he did it the way he wanted."

On most nights, the revamped squad now seemed able to score at will, anytime, from anywhere. Often, mere seconds into the game, opposing players would feel their knees go weak as they realized just what they were up against. Many games were all but over moments after the opening tip. "We'd start the game by working the ball in and out real fast," said Inman Jackson. "Then we'd hit on a dunk shot. Then the other team would say, 'Gosh, these guys can do whatever they want with the ball.'"

The Globetrotters finished their second year with a 145-13 record, and then topped that by going 151-13 in the 1929–30 season. Unfortunately, victories did not at first translate into more money for the financially strapped team. It often seemed that the struggling Globetrotters' only trouble-free moments occurred while they were breezing up and down the court. But even at those times the stark sight of a half-empty gym (not to mention the

sound of their half-empty stomachs) was there to remind them of their situation.

The Great Depression, brought on by the stock market crash of 1929, seemed, by 1931, to have emptied everyone's pockets of all but dust. Few people had heard of the fledgling barnstorming unit from Chicago, and even fewer had the money to go see a basketball game. Abe Saperstein's dream of a world-traveling, world-famous team had been born in a different time, the Roaring Twenties, a time when tuxedoed men strutted with their dates to the Savoy Ballroom to, as Cab Calloway said, "be entertained." Abruptly, times had changed.

But Saperstein did not let his dream die. To make ends meet, he booked more games than it seemed humanly possible for his hungry and perpetually road-weary team to play. "We often played three games in two days on one meal consisting of hamburgers," Saperstein said.

Saperstein's demanding schedule was not enough to drive his players away. Aware of the crippling poverty engulfing the country, the players felt lucky to have a job at all. The depression, instead of tearing the team apart, actually fused it more tightly together than ever, as Abe's brother Harry recalled: "The players stayed with Abe through thick and thin, but I've got to make mention of this: This was the early '30s and these were Depression years. Don't lose sight of the fact that a one dollar bill looked mighty, mighty big. You couldn't buy a job for a hundred dollars, and anything that smacked of fifteen dollars a week or more, you had to grab onto, so the black players' future, if you could call it that, laid in the Globetrotters succeeding, to some extent, so their paycheck could grow with the team."

Sometimes Saperstein lent his salesman's golden tongue to the purpose of renewing the players' faith in the future of the team. Once in a while, however, even his confidence wavered. Near the end of one long and financially fruitless tour through the West, Saperstein poured out all his doubts and fears to Inman Jackson. The two men were walking at dusk down the main street of a small British Columbia town called Lonesome Woman Gulch. Saperstein told Jackson that he had been a fool to think the Globetrotters could make it. He had been a fool to convince the players to throw their lots in with a dreamer. It just was not working, he said.

Jackson did not reply at first. The wind blew down the empty street. Jackson pointed at the snowcapped mountains looming on the horizon. "Maybe things aren't going so good right now, boss," he said. "But isn't the scenery wonderful?" Nothing else could be said. Saperstein and the Globetrotters kept on trying.

The scenery was not always so nice. Not long after the visit to Lonesome Woman Gulch, the team, traveling toward a game in Miles City, ran smack into a raging Montana snowstorm. On an icy back road, Saperstein lost control of his Model T Ford and the old car careened into a ditch. The team's new second car, piloted by Inman Jackson, did not fare much better, slipping and skidding and finally sinking deep into an enormous roadside snowbank. Though there appeared to be no refuge in any direction from the blinding, wind-whipped snow, the team forged on down the road on foot. They had no choice. As it turned out, this desperate persistence, a specialty of the depression-era Globetrotters (along with some luck, another specialty), helped spirit the team to safety.

*Barred from the major professional leagues until the late 1940s and 1950s, black athletes had no choice but to earn their living on the road. The Cincinnati Tigers of baseball's Negro leagues posed in 1936 in front of the bus in which they barnstormed the country. Saperstein was also a dominant figure in the Negro leagues, acting as the primary agent for booking teams into major-league ballparks, for which he received a substantial cut of 40 percent of the gate.*

They came upon a ramshackle sheep farm, manned by a grizzled shepherd who immediately offered them shelter. The miracle revealed itself as a mixed blessing, however, when the man ushered the team to the only place he had for them to wait out the storm, which would rage on for three more days. Many years later, the miserable bleating of the team's dim-witted shackmates still echoed in Abe Saperstein's mind. "There were fourteen guys and nine sheep in that shack for three days," Saperstein lamented. "When people remark that I've got a soft racket with the Globetrotters I ask them if they've ever inhaled for three days in a 20-by-14 room with fourteen guys and nine sheep."

In no way did Saperstein have an easy racket. He was, however, immune to the greatest hardship that his players had to withstand. The color of his skin granted this immunity. Throughout much of the country, Jim Crow laws, which were designed to segregate blacks from whites, still prevailed. In those places where Jim Crow was not written into law, it was still, as often as not, practiced. As they traveled the land, the Globetrotters paid the price for this institutionalized racism. Towns throughout the West and Midwest would welcome the team into the hometown gym for a game and then refuse the black players lodging in their hotels. As this happened again and again, the players were made ever more acutely aware that they were living in a land that did not want them.

"Those times were pretty rough," Inman Jackson said. "Abe would try to get us into a decent hotel but sometimes he couldn't. I remember in Bismarck, North Dakota, there was an old colored couple that would let us sleep on cots on the floor. Another time Abe argued with a hotel manager to let us in. He wouldn't so Abe had to rent a room, and we waited until late at night. Then I went up the fire escape and got myself a good night's sleep. But it was always a problem."

An incident in Omaha, Nebraska, recalled by Globetrotter Bernie Price, further illustrates the kind of suffering the weary team had to endure. "After the game," Price said, "a boy came on by and said, 'I got a place for you.' So we go by this big fine hotel. The kid on the desk must have been young or new on the job because he gave us rooms, but about 4 o'clock in the morning we had to get up and get out. So we got in the bus and drove on down toward the town where we were playing next." Price concluded the story with words that seemed to capture the desolate ache of homelessness that never seemed to leave the players: "We drove all night, just kept on going."

Price concurred with Jackson that the owner of the Globetrotters fought as hard as he could against the segregation practices the team ran into. But, as one man alone against the custom and law of much of the country, his efforts amounted to little. "Saperstein would intercede for us," said Price, "but hell, there wasn't anything he could do about it."

Saperstein slept with his players on more than one occasion in the only place that some towns would allow blacks to stay—the town jail. He also once experienced something vaguely akin to what his players routinely suffered when the police kicked him out of an all-black hotel in Atlanta. But he was never remotely near being in the same situation as his players. Whether it came in the solid shape of a strictly enforced Jim Crow law or in the more nebulous form of a local townsperson's caustic look, the assault on the players' dignity never ended. Inman Jackson remembered those looks, full at the same time of fear and hatred. "We felt we always had to act twice as good as anybody else," he said, "because people were always watching us."

One place where the players had little trouble proving themselves twice as good as anyone else was on the court. They sprinkled long strings of routine wins with stunning routs that had in them the unmistakable flavor of vengeance. A game in Woodfibre, British Columbia, started as one of these merciless beatings and ended up as a turning point in the team's history.

Before the opening tap, as the two teams warmed up, hecklers in the stands loosed a drunken torrent of abuse in the direction of the Globetrotter players. The players, usually able to keep their emotions in check, decided, for whatever reason, that enough was enough. Runt Pullins gathered his teammates around him and, with seven quick words—"Let's pour it on these wise guys"—triggered an ungodly basketball massacre.

Late in the game, with the score 112-5, the ugly fans began to get uglier. At that time, fan violence, particularly racially motivated fan violence, was by no means unknown in professional basketball. Even in a supposedly cosmopolitan place like New York City, for example, a Jewish player named Moe Goldman recalled anti-Semitic fans routinely throwing drinks at him as he ran downcourt and burning him "with a lighted cigarette as I stood there to take the ball out."

Thus, in a gym in a small town in the Canadian wilderness, surrounded by a crowd of burly, irate, liquor-fueled loggers on the brink of violence, the Globetrotters knew they were in trouble. They knew something had to be done.

In *Elevating the Game: The History and Aesthetics of Black Men in Basketball*, writer Nelson George points out that in the 1930s in the United States there could be few things in sports as potentially incendiary as "five Black men rolling into a Midwestern town, kicking ass, and getting paid." He further points out that the aspect of the Globetrotters' game that would eventually make them world famous, their clowning, first arose as a way to

*Saperstein offers his team some tactical advice. His genius, however, was as a promoter and entrepreneur, not as a coach.*

ameliorate such situations. "Clowning Black men," writes George, "have always been more popular in this country than stern, no-nonsense brothers."

As tension mounted during that game in the town of Woodfibre, the Globetrotters decided it was time to try to become a little more popular. Runt Pullins dribbled the ball through his legs, smiling broadly, then passed to Inman Jackson, who whipped a behind-the-back pass to Kid Oliver, who tossed the ball in the air and caught it on the back of his neck, then let it roll down his arm. The complexion of the game seemed to change almost instantly. What before had been a crushing, menacing rout was now a harmless, circuslike exhibition of what seemed to the fans wondrous, otherworldly skills. At a time when most players could barely dribble at all and did so only when absolutely necessary, Runt Pullins was dribbling and tap-dancing at the same time. The fans were held in thrall by the barnstorming team's tricks. Perhaps more importantly, the wide, vaudevillian smiles now plastered on the faces of the Trotters communicated to the white audience that, though they could indeed play some serious ball, the Harlem Globetrotters meant absolutely, positively, no harm to anyone. By the end of the game, laughter reigned.

When, over the next few games, he realized that his team could still win while hamming it up a little, Saperstein began to encourage the clowning. For one thing, many of the *reems*— the Globetrotter term for all ballhandling tricks, gags, and clowning—allowed the team to rest their tired legs while the game was in progress. For example, as Runt Pullins went into his tap-dancing/dribbling routine, the other four players on the floor did not even have to move. Also, the gags helped keep the score a little closer, making it appear that the hometown team was not as overmatched as they really were. This pleased the hometown fans and also encouraged a return engagement, as a soundly thrashed team might not be eager to invite the Globetrotters back. But the simplest reason for Saperstein's increasing support of the reems was that he saw that the fans loved it.

The Globetrotters played a game at this time in a gym in Williamsburg, Iowa, that had a red-hot, fully stoked, potbellied wood stove at each end line. Late in the game, Kid Oliver leaped for a rebound and was jostled in the air and sent sprawling out of bounds. He landed, rear end first, on one of the stoves, and his red, white, and blue shorts caught on fire. As he ran screaming to the locker room, with flames licking up at his back, the fans exploded with laughter, thinking it all a part of the Globetrotters' routine.

The spectacle gave Saperstein a clearer picture of how his team was going to climb toward the fame he had always envisioned for them. "Kid," Saperstein cracked with considerable giddiness in the smoky locker room, "you're undoubtedly the hottest player I've had since the team started barnstorming." The team owner, who was beginning to develop a preternatural sense of just when to make a gesture to cool a player's rebellious indignance, then slid the still-distressed Kid Oliver a crisp $50 bill.

As the reems slowly worked their way into the team's nightly act, Saperstein did make sure the Trotters concentrated on what was most important. "First we win," he said, "then we clown." He knew that the gateway to widespread recognition still lay mainly in continued on-court dominance. He also seemed to have within him an overpowering need to always be on the winning side. Tony Lavelli, a close friend of Saperstein's, once said of the Trotter head man, "I have learned it is best to stay away from him after his team loses. He is downcast, morbid, and just plain hurt."

These were not emotions Saperstein felt very often. The upbeat leader presided as the Globetrotters continued to stomp their opposition, no matter what the circumstance. In Harlem, Montana, the team played in a drained swimming pool, stalling for time in the first half as they struggled uphill in the direction of their basket, which was at the top of the sloping shallow end. At halftime, the teams switched ends, and the Globetrotters coasted downhill to victory.

In Des Plaines, Illinois, the hometown team got free for easy baskets by running the Trotters into "picks" set by huge pillars in the middle of the court. The Globetrotters slowed the game down, giving

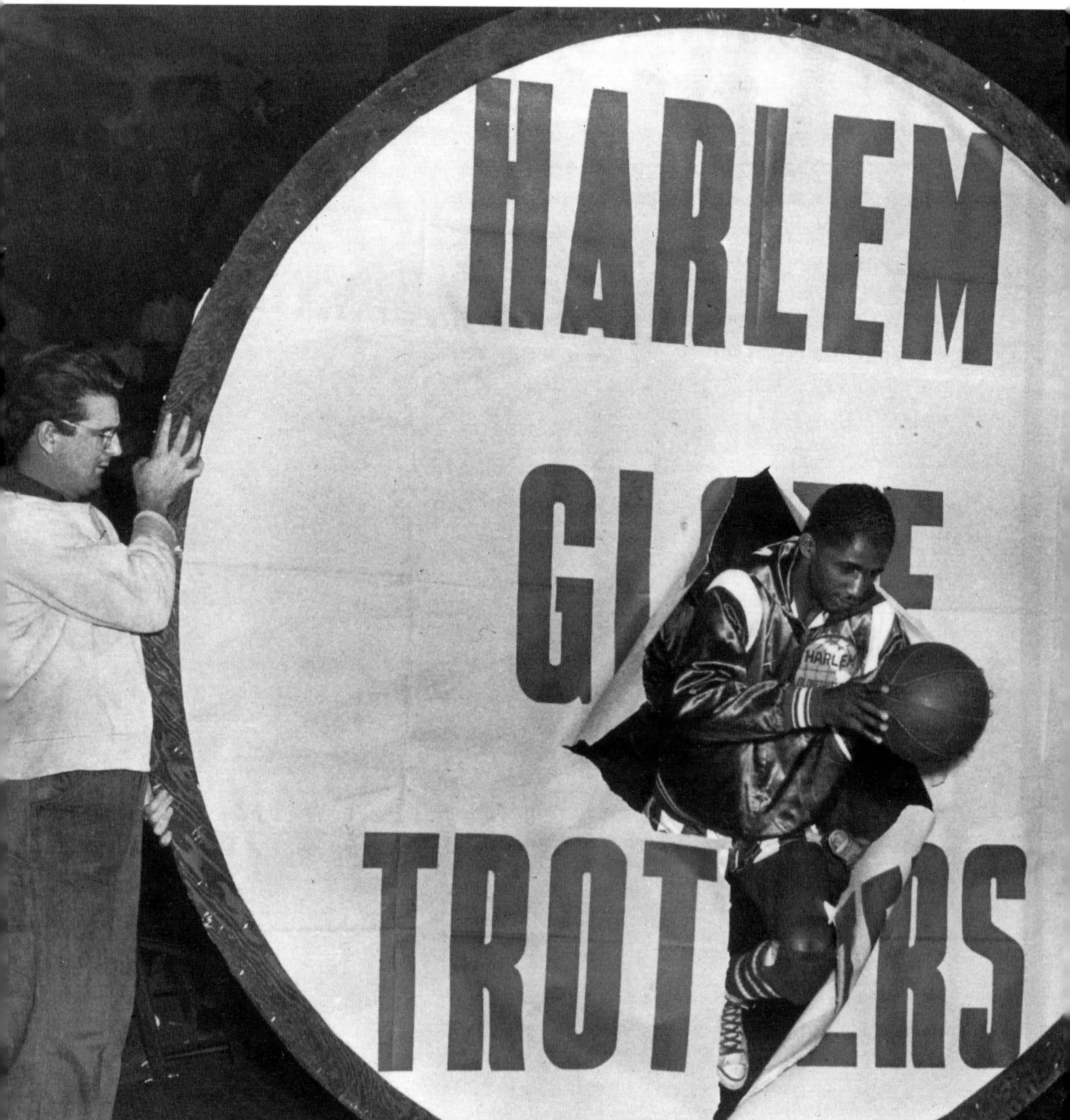
HARLEM

# 4

## World Champions

I N 1939 THE Harlem Globetrotters rolled into Chicago with a purpose. The first-ever World Tournament was being held at Chicago Stadium, and the Globetrotters saw it as their big chance to fight their way out of a decade of relative obscurity. Finally, after years of toying with small-town all-star teams, Abe Saperstein's players would get a chance to prove themselves against the best pro teams in the land. The chaotic mix of teams at the first World Tournament included, among others, pro-league powerhouses such as the Oshkosh All-Stars and the Sheboygan Redskins, the legendary Original Celtics and the downright fearsome Harlem Rens, a home-town favorite called the Chicago Harmons, an over-matched pickup team called the New York Yankees, and, for comic relief, the fake-beard-wearing House of David hoopsters.

The Globetrotters got the tournament started with a 41-33 win over the Fort Wayne Harvesters to advance to the second round. The Trotters then bounced the powerful Chicago Harmons from the

*Breaking through: ballhandling wizard Marques Haynes leads the Harlem Globetrotters onto the court.*

tournament, 31-25. In the next round, the semifinals, the Rens stood in their path.

The Rens, for most people who paid attention to professional basketball, were *the* black team of the 1920s and 1930s. Founded in 1923 by a black immigrant from Saint Kitts in the Caribbean named Robert Douglas, the Rens had been a success from their earliest games in the Renaissance Ballroom in Harlem. Unlike the Globetrotters in the early years, the Rens made money. The Rens also differed from the Globetrotters in that, since they were based in New York City, the nation's hotbed of professional basketball at that time, they were able early on to prove their mettle against top eastern teams like the Original Celtics and the Philadelphia Sphas. Their quick rise to prominence allowed them to pick from hundreds of black players hungry to earn a spot on the team. One Ren player recalled the team's tryouts: "Remember, this was the only well-known, premier black team in the country, so they would have the best black players from all over come in. Maybe they'd have a hundred, two hundred guys out **there** and picked the best eight."

By 1939 the Rens had been at the top of the basketball world for longer than any team around, save for their old rivals, the Original Celtics. Unlike the Celtics, however, who were upset in the second round of the World Tournament, the Rens showed no signs of decline. In fact, as they breezed into their semifinal match with the Globetrotters, they appeared to have put together one of their strongest units ever. Joining veterans such as big, bruising Wee Willie Smith and Hall of Fame center Charles T. "Tarzan" Cooper were younger players such as Johnny Isaacs (whom Robert Douglas claimed "had more natural ability than any man to have ever played for me") and a 21-year-old scorer in the first year of a Hall of Fame professional career, William "Pop" Gates. Of Gates, Douglas simply said,

"Nothing could stop him."

Having advanced farther in the tournament than many had thought they could go, the Globetrotters gave the Rens what turned out to be their toughest challenge of the year. The game was a low-scoring one. The Rens played a so-called eastern style of basketball, which meant they liked to slow the ball down and pound it in to their big men. The Globetrotters, proponents of a more wide-open game, could not keep the more experienced Rens from controlling the tempo. But the Trotters played valiantly, staying in the game until the end, losing finally by only four, 27-23; it was the closest to defeat that the Rens would come that year. With relative ease, Robert Douglas's team rolled over the NBL champs, the Oshkosh All-Stars, in the championship game, 34-25, to become the first "world" champions. The Globetrotters gained third place in the tournament, and even greater respect, by topping the Sheboygan Redskins in the consolation game.

The Globetrotters reaped the benefits of their successful showing at the World Tournament the following season as an increased awareness of the team bolstered attendance at their games. The team, led by Duke Cumberland and a young streak-shooting guard named Sonny Boswell, steamrolled into the 1940 World Tournament on the wings of their best record ever, 159-8.

The Globetrotters crushed the unfortunate Kenosha Royals, 50-26, in the opening round. The team's next game would not be so easy. The tournament bracket pitted them against the team they would have to beat sooner or later, but the Trotters had not thought it would have to be so soon. As 20,000 fans buzzed with excitement, the Trotters took a few jittery pregame warm-up shots and nervously perused their opponents. The confident Rens, garbed in flashy warm-up suits with the words

*Doc Tally of the House of David basketball team. The bearded barnstormers (there was also a House of David baseball team) rivaled the Globetrotters as a draw.*

"World Champions" emblazoned on the back, assaulted the basket at the other end of the court with deadeye long-range bombs and rattling slam dunks. The Globetrotters retreated to the locker room just before the game was to begin, their confidence badly shaken.

Inman Jackson, the hoary veteran of the team's toughest years, gazed around the locker room at the looks of underconfidence and downright fear on the faces of his younger teammates. He sensed that it was time to do something. He had been battling in obscurity for over a decade, the toughest decade the team would ever live through. He had fought too hard and for too long to let this opportunity pass. The team had to reach out and grab for glory right then. Jackson began to speak, and as he spoke the fire crept back into the eyes of all the Globetrotters. By the time he stopped speaking, the team was up, clapping, shouting, flexing their muscular arms and legs. By the end of the speech, the team was ready. The time had come for the Harlem Globetrotters to prove to the world how good they were. "Some of the guys were nervous," Jackson said years later. "But I told them that the Rens could only play 5 men at a time, the same as us." As for the game, Jackson simply said, "We got over being nervous and we beat them. After that, we knew we could win the tournament."

After toppling the Rens, the Globetrotters beat the Syracuse Reds to advance to the championship game. The Chicago Bruins of the NBL, led by high-scoring guard Wibs Kautz and a towering six-foot nine-inch center with a surprisingly soft shooting touch named Mike Novak, remained the only team left for the Trotters to beat. The Bruins, on a roll that had seen them breeze through the tournament, beating their opponents by an average of 9 points a game, took control of the game early. The Globetrotters managed to shackle Kautz, but they had no

*As a member of the world-champion Rens squad of 1939, William "Pop" Gates was one of the Globetrotters' foremost rivals, but he later starred for the Globetrotters as player-coach from 1951 to 1955.*

one tall enough to effectively guard Novak, who led the way for the Bruins as they forged ahead in the first half.

With only a few minutes remaining in the contest, the Bruins had what was, considering the low score of the game, a fairly sizable five-point lead. Then Sonny Boswell began to fire away. A Boswell net-tickling bomb from near half-court highlighted a furious rally that would knot the score by the end of regulation. In overtime Boswell continued to hit on improbable set shots, and the Globetrotters eked out a two-point win that crowned them the kings of the basketball world.

Abe Saperstein knew a potential promotional bonanza when he saw one. He revamped the team uniforms, sewing the words "World Champions" on the back and making them the star-spangled red, white, and blue garments that the Globetrotters still wear today. Saperstein also bought a new bus for the team, raised the Trotters' salaries, and rented an 11-room home office in Chicago. The days of operating a business out of the backseat of his Model T Ford were over.

Saperstein did not stop there. To further juice up the Globetrotter act, he added halftime entertainment to the bill of many of the team's games, hiring jugglers, singers, tap dancers, and table tennis players, among others. He also saw that although the team was now more well known than ever, it

*One of the unsung black pioneers of professional basketball, Charles "Tarzan" Cooper played and coached for more than 20 years with the Rens and other black teams.*

was not as famous as it could be. The Trotters had established themselves as the best professional team around, but in 1940 such a distinction was not that great a claim to fame.

In those days professional basketball lagged far behind college basketball in fan appeal. Whereas the best college players were renowned nationwide, the top professional players were revered, if at all, only in the cities where they plied their trade. Saperstein realized all this and wisely set up a game between the Globetrotters and an all-star team made up of the best college players in the country. On November 30, 1940, 22,000 fans, even more than had shown up for the World Tournament game between the Rens and the Trotters, packed Chicago Stadium to watch a thrilling overtime game, won by the College All-Stars, 44-42. For once, Abe Saperstein did not get angry about a loss. He could see that his dream was coming true.

"That was the night we came into our own, the night we won a million followers and really started going places," he later said about the game. "The fact that we almost beat one of the greatest collections of basketball talent ever gathered on one floor proved to the public that there was such a team as the Globetrotters and that it was not only good, but a crowd-pleaser."

The Globetrotters' surging popularity, coupled with the gradual demise of the Rens, meant that Saperstein's team now had their pick of most of the top black players in the country. Saperstein's myriad connections and friendships forged over his many years on the road formed a vast, nationwide scouting network for the team. If there was a promising black basketball player anywhere in the country, it was not long before Abe Saperstein knew that athlete's name.

Soon after the Globetrotters' impressive performance against the collegians, Abe Saperstein got a call from a friend named Winfield Welch. Welch had been watching a group of Negro leagues baseball players fooling around at a gym in Fort Benning, Georgia, after one of their games had been rained out. The team's first baseman, Welch told Saperstein, was playing the wrong sport. With his huge hands and freakishly long arms, the man could whip a basketball around as if it were a grapefruit. And there was something else too. Simply put, the man was funny. Goose Tatum was his name.

Saperstein took Welch's advice and gave Goose Tatum a tryout. The young athlete was still new to the game of basketball, and it showed. During the tryout Tatum, having mastered none of the fundamental skills of basketball, struggled against more experienced players, and at times he looked awkward, confused, and downright clumsy. He was not, to put it mildly, an overnight success. But Saperstein saw something he liked in Tatum. Possibly Saperstein was able to see some untapped grace lurking beneath all the fumbled passes and missed shots.

Tatum viewed the surprising result of his less-than-spectacular tryout in a different, more direct way. "There were so many others who played better than me. Guess they left me on the squad because I wanted to play so badly."

The new Globetrotter named Reece "Goose" Tatum was born on May 3, 1921, in Eldorado, Arkansas, one of seven children of a Methodist preacher. An athlete from his earliest days, he got his nickname catching touchdown passes in a pickup game, where a boisterous spectator pointed and shouted, "Look at that old goose fly!" Tatum exhibited his greatest potential in baseball, however, and while he was still a teenager he left home, beginning a life spent almost exclusively on the road, to play on a semipro team in a mill town in the Ozark Mountains. There he was approached by scouts from the Negro leagues and was soon playing first

*The Rens and Original Celtics battle for rebounding position. In the 1920s and 1930s, their rivalry was considered basketball's greatest, but by the outbreak of World War II, the Globetrotters were poised to challenge for the title of the world's best basketball team.*

base for a team called, portentously, the Cincinnati Clowns.

The baseball scouting report for Tatum, if such a thing ever existed, would have said about the young player: good field, weak hit. The report might have

the 1942–43 season. Divisions soon formed along seemingly racial lines between the former Trotters and their white teammates, many of whom, ironically, had been members of the Chicago Bruins squad vanquished by the Trotters at the 1940 World Tournament. The Trotter players, however, denied that the dissension was racially based, instead blaming it on a battle between Boswell and Mike Novak over who was the team's primary offensive player. "I think it was a matter of egos," said Bernie Price. "I don't think it was racial."

But Price and the other black players on the Studebakers did encounter racial prejudice from the fans. Remembering Oshkosh, Wisconsin, as a particularly bad place to play, Price said, "They didn't like us up there. I imagine it was because we were black. The fans used to shoot staples at us."

Meanwhile, Saperstein tried to make do with what he could, using many older and less-talented players to fill out his team. In 1942 he signed a big center out of Iowa named Bob Karstens. As it happened, Karstens was white, the only white player (besides Saperstein, in the very early years) to ever play for the team. He had a flair for entertaining that fit in well with the Globetrotters' act. He has been credited with inventing a gag, still in use by the team today, in which a ball weighted in a lopsided way to make it bounce crazily is switched for the regular ball. This information should be taken with a grain of salt, as Karstens is also credited with starting the Globetrotter Magic Circle act, which clearly was in practice, albeit in a rough form, as early as 1931, long before Karstens was there. Karstens lasted about 14 months with the team.

The end of World War II marked the beginning of a time of economic prosperity in America. The Globetrotters, just as they had struggled when the nation had struggled, would begin to prosper as the nation began to prosper. Fresh from his three-year

stint in the Air Force, Goose Tatum would lead the way.  From the moment, prior to the game's start, when Goose Tatum shuffled onto the court wearing an undersized jacket to highlight his unusually long arms (the Goose had a "wingspan" that measured 84 inches from fingertip to fingertip) to the moment when he added an exclamation point to the game by nonchalantly sinking a half-court hook shot at the buzzer, Goose had the fans in the palm of his gargantuan hand.

Saperstein felt that Tatum captivated his audience on the strength of his uncanny comic timing. Said the Globetrotter boss, "A lot of people try to be funny but they fall flat on their faces because they lack the sixth sense that tells a genius like Tatum

*Though Sweetwater Clifton (left) and Goose Tatum (right) helped carry the Globetrotters to their greatest heights, they also experienced the downside of life on the team.  Both would fall out with Saperstein over the owner's business practices.*

precisely the time to punch across a particular caper." Right from the start, in the pregame Magic Circle, Goose outshone all his flashy teammates, not so much by any wondrous trick but by that comic timing and by using his elastic face and rubbery limbs to make himself seem larger than life. "A true pantomime artist," wrote a reporter for *Life* magazine at the time, "he expresses himself not in speech but in movement." To many of the fans, Tatum's performance went past art and into the realm of magic. "He looked," thought an amazed 11-year-old kid named Meadow George Lemon seeing Tatum play for the first time, "like his arms and legs weren't even attached to his body."

Tatum took over a game like a crazed captain grabbing the helm of a ship. On the court (as well as off the court, as he would later prove) Tatum had no interest in steering things in a simple line from point A to point B. Goose liked taking detours. He would range into the audience to snag a man's hat, then swagger onto the court, the lid perched rakishly on his noggin, and call for the ball. He would then fake his defender in about seven different directions, until the man was practically tied into knots, at which point Tatum would crown his stooge with the pilfered hat, yawn grandly, and score with a flat-footed, roundhouse hook shot. Then he would strut back on defense, pausing to tango with the referee and swing over to the sidelines to borrow someone's camera for a few preening self-portraits and to slap hands with as many fans as he could, and everyone would start to get the feeling they were part of the crazy ride. Tatum led the fans from point A to point B, but not without a little side trip to points J and X and D and G and Z.

Even Tatum's teammates got swept along in the lead clown's madness. "Goose was a genius," said a Globetrotter teammate named Leon Hillard. "There may never be anybody quite like him again.

He had a feeling for his audience, for the situation, that was unbelievable. He could be so funny, we'd all be laughing right on the court."

"You laughed at Goose just looking at him," added Marques Haynes. "No one will ever match him. You laugh at him now just thinking about him." Decades after it happened, a smile still came to Haynes's face when he thought about the Globetrotters' first trip to Hawaii. At the start of that Hawaii game, which marked for the team the beginning of a new era of genuine round-the-world globetrotting, Goose Tatum sauntered onto the court wearing a grass hula skirt. "He got in the pivot and started making those gangly, crazy moves with that skirt on and people were laughing so hard they were crying. He had players on the bench falling over each other." Haynes added with a smile, "He's the best I've seen in all my years."

# 5

## "Are You Kidding, Mr. Saperstein?"

W HEN GOOSE TATUM passed the ball to Marques Oreole Haynes, the laughter rocking the building trickled to a stop, replaced by silent, breathless awe. Right in front of everyone's eyes, Haynes was changing the way basketball was played. Throughout the first 50 years of the game, dribbling had been used, for the most part, only when absolutely necessary. Coaches taught their teams to move the ball solely by way of the pass. Someone who dribbled more than even two or three times in a row was roundly condemned as a terrible ball hog. Marques Haynes could dribble two or three times a second and, while he was doing it, could weave in and out of all five defenders like a fly eluding the grasping, arthritic fingers of an old and tired man.

He shattered defenses with his dribbling. As he dribbled, he always seemed to be on the brink of splitting cleanly in two, so forceful were his body fakes, but always he kept complete control, eluding, ducking, hesitating, stutter stepping, faking, blasting forward, skittering away, pausing, lulling, spinning, gliding, the ball always pounding out a machine-gun rhythm on the court. And whenever Haynes wanted to, he could practically sting the air

*"Talk to serious ballplayers about the Trotters' impact on their game and [Marques] Haynes is the name that recurs," writes Nelson George in* Elevating the Game: The History and Aesthetics of Black Men in Basketball.

with a sharp, quick burst toward the basket and score. In his style of play he resembled alto saxophonist Charlie Parker, who was at that time revolutionizing jazz by flooding his songs with a virtual torrent of notes both ferocious and practically bursting with joy. Jazz would never be the same, and neither would basketball. Musicians would follow the path that Parker blazed. Basketball players followed Haynes's path.

Walt Hazzard, who led UCLA to the first of their many championships in 1964 before going on to star in the NBA, marks the first time he saw Marques Haynes play as the beginning of his basketball education. "Up until then I had never seen anybody dribble the ball like that before," said Hazzard. "He'd be on the floor, on one knee and people couldn't take the ball from him. . . . I was 7 or 8 years old, and Marques had an immediate impact on me."

Hazzard was not alone. Nearly two decades later, Haynes's ability to dominate the action from the guard position impressed a young student of the game named Earvin Johnson. "Marques Haynes was my hero when it came to dribbling," said the man who would come to be known as Magic. "He would get lower and lower until he was lying on the floor, still dribbling the basketball. . . . Marques never looked at the ball; he always kept it away because every time the defender made a motion one way or the other, Marques would be able to evade him just as quick."

Haynes, hailing from Sand Springs, Oklahoma, where he was born in or around the year 1925, joined the Globetrotters in 1946. When he was a young child, his sister made a habit of taking him to her basketball practices. Marques had to wait for her on the sidelines. With nothing better to do, he started dribbling. As he got older, his small frame excluded him from many of the neighborhood games. Again he was relegated to the sidelines.

*He could score as well as clown: Goose Tatum gets loose for two against the College All-Stars in 1952.*

Rather than giving up, he kept practicing the dribble. By junior high, he still had not grown enough to be anything more than a mascot for the school team. Finally, in 11th grade, he made the varsity team; slowly, he worked his way into the starting lineup. By the end of his senior year, he was a star, leading his team to the National Negro High School Championship in Tuskegee, Alabama.

He went on from there to star at Langston University, an all-black school in central Oklahoma. During his years there, Haynes led the team to a Globetrotter-like 112-3 record. Heeding Coach Zip

*By 1950, the Globetrotters had begun to live up to their name, establishing themselves as a popular act overseas as well as across the United States. On July 31 of that year, they were photographed as they disembarked from the ocean liner* Mauretania *upon their return from engagements in Europe and Africa.*

Gayles's plea to play a strictly fundamental game, Haynes kept his dribbling forays to a minimum. Only once did he, as he put it, "go into my act." In his junior year, he punctuated Langston's conference championship game win over a cocky Southern University squad by dribbling out the final two and one-half minutes of the game, eluding his opponents while whipping the audience into a roaring frenzy. "People went crazy," said Haynes. "They got louder and louder." Coins and pieces of clothing and pages of ripped-up programs rained down onto the court as Haynes skidded and slithered and danced away the final seconds of the game.

At the end of the following year, the Langston team played host to the Harlem Globetrotters. Before the game, Globetrotter captain Duke Cumberland took Zip Gayles aside and assured him, "We won't beat you by a whole lot." As it turned out, the Globetrotters would not beat Langston University at all. Haynes scored 26 points to lead his team to a stunning 74-70 win.

The Globetrotters offered Haynes a spot on their team before the sweat from the game had dried, but the youngster had his priorities in order. "I was right on top of getting a degree," he later recalled. "My mother would have killed me if I had left school."

A few months later, college diploma in hand, Haynes joined a Globetrotter farm team called the Kansas City Stars. After dribbling circles around the competition in the minor leagues for a few weeks, he joined the big club. Describing his first year with the team with an understatement typical of his modest nature, Haynes said, "I created somewhat of an uproar with my dribbling and ball-handling."

In the late 1940s and early 1950s, Haynes was the best player on a team that could hold their own with any other team in the world. After the big 1948 win over the Minneapolis Lakers in Chicago Stadium, the Globetrotters began an annual series against a team of the nation's best college players. Against a 1950 college all-star team that included future Hall of Famers Paul Arizin and Bob Cousy, the Globetrotters did, basically, anything they wanted to do on the court. Goose Tatum flicked in shots from a sitting position. Two players played keep away from the college boys as the three other Trotters ambled into the stands to sign autographs. Another time four Globetrotters on the court grabbed newspapers from a vendor in the stands and sprawled on the hardwood to read as Haynes ran his one-man offense. Haynes later befuddled a three-some of college all-stars, including the wizardly Cousy, to such an extent that they crashed into each other as he skittered in for an easy deuce. Sweetwater Clifton got himself into the act, rolling the ball through his defender's legs to Babe Pressley. Pressley rolled it back to Clifton, who then laid it down on the floor, as if to surrender. The college all-star dove for the ball, but Pressley was quicker, nudging a pass with his toe to Tatum for a stuff. Haynes was named the most valuable player as the Trotters took 13 of the 18 games in the series.

In Saperstein's mind, the Harlem Globetrotters were ready to conquer the world. In the summer of 1950 he dreamed up a 73-game trip through Western Europe and North Africa. His business manager took one glance at the lofty plan and asked, "Are you kidding, Mr. Saperstein?" Saperstein disregarded the man's advice and the Globetrotters, at long last, began to truly globetrot.

In nearly every place the Globetrotters visited, basketball was all but unknown. In England, for example, where the Globetrotters kicked off their tour, basketball, if known at all, was thought of somewhat disparagingly as a game little girls played. Saperstein said of the games in London's Wembley Stadium, "I thought we'd take a whipping here. I expected 10,000 people." After the first game at Wembley was televised, however, a rush for tickets ensued that brought 50,000 fans to the game on the second night.

The London newspapers were the first to publish the rave reviews that would follow the team wherever they went all summer long, with one article proclaiming, "Amazing, uncanny, thrilling—the finest sporting spectacle in the world!" The director of the stadium, Sir Arthur J. Elvin, said, "Abe Saperstein will go down in British sporting history as the man who made Britain basketball conscious."

Saperstein could not bask in the kudos of titled British stadium owners for long. During the summer of the Globetrotters' first overseas tour, the young NBA, which had formed in 1949 as a merger between the Basketball Association of America and the NBL, was preparing to bring black players into the league. This did not sit well with Saperstein, who by all accounts enjoyed having a monopoly on top black basketball talent.

Saperstein held a position of power with regard to the NBA. Struggling mightily to stay afloat despite generally atrocious fan turnout, the fledgling league had turned to Saperstein and his Globetrotters for help. The Globetrotters, now basking in the first powerful blasts of fame, were often called on to prop up the NBA by playing a doubleheader bill with an NBA game. On nights when the Globetrotters played on their bill, the NBA teams got a rare good turnout. Saperstein promised to yank the helping hand away should any NBA team attempt to sign a black player.

Saperstein did not want his monopoly on the best black basketball talent to end. It was good for his business to have such a monopoly. But there was more to the issue than just good business. Saperstein seemed to fancy himself both a benevolent leader and a helper of downtrodden black men. As strange as it may now seem—keeping in mind that the man wanted to be the sole owner, in effect, of the rights to all black basketball players in America—Saperstein saw himself as a great help to African Americans. "I'd like to contribute something to better understanding between whites and Negroes," he once said.

The enigma that was Abe Saperstein in many ways centers the story of the Harlem Globetrotters. It seems that, from his own perspective, Saperstein did care about the welfare of African Americans. But that caring took a paternalistic shape in which

*Sweetwater Clifton of the Globetrotters drives left around Irwin Dambrot of the College All-Stars in an April 18, 1950, contest between the two squads. The Globetrotters won this one, 72-59.*

Saperstein always held all the power and in which blacks never were able to gain the full measure of dignity that was their due as human beings. When Chuck Cooper, who played briefly with the Globetrotters before joining the Boston Celtics, was signed to an NBA contract in 1950, breaking the league color line, one Globetrotter remarked, "Ol' Abe sure pitched a bitch when he heard about that. He knew then he could no longer be the great white father."

The first direct hit to Saperstein's team came when the New York Knicks signed Sweetwater Clifton. Clifton, increasingly dissatisfied with Saperstein's treatment of him, bristled at the fact that Saperstein was paying the college all-stars more than he was paying the Globetrotters themselves. "I became a little peeved at him," said Clifton of Saperstein, "and decided I was going to go someplace else." Aware that the Knicks coveted his star center's services, Saperstein told Clifton he would sell him to the NBA team. Clifton received half of the $5,000 Saperstein said the Knicks paid in the deal, but it turned out that Saperstein lied about the selling price.

"I believed him because I thought everybody was honest," said Clifton. "That's the way I was raised, to take a person at their word." As Clifton was to learn years later, Saperstein had sold him to the Knicks for approximately $25,000, pocketing all but the relative pittance of $2,500 he had dishonestly foisted off on the player. "But you know, you got to take the bitter with the sweet," recalled Clifton, revealing a remarkable ability to shrug off the injuries of a sometimes unjust world.

This quality served him well during his time as a pioneer black player in the predominantly white NBA. Clifton found he had to stifle the freewheeling style of play he had come to love as a Globetrotter. "They didn't want me to be fancy," Clifton said. "I felt like I was sacrificing . . . and I don't think other guys would have done that. Being the first in something, you don't want to do anything that'll mess it up for someone else." Knicks teammate Carl Braun recalled that there were times when "Sweets took an extra bump because he was black."

But only once in a frequently exasperating NBA career did Clifton's expansive patience wear thin. During an exhibition game against the Celtics, Clifton found himself matched up against a foulmouthed and racist reserve center named Bob Harris. "I did a little Globetrotter stuff to him," remembered Clifton, "and he said where he came from people didn't do him like that. I'm not gonna say exactly what he said, but it made me kinda angry." A witness to the ensuing fight, Celtics star Ed Macauley, said, "Clifton was awesome. He doubled up his fists and used them like hammers." Said Clifton, "After that I didn't have any more trouble with anybody."

The breaking of the color line did not seem to have an effect on the Globetrotters at first. They kept rolling over their competition and scoring big at the box office. In April 1951, they drew a crowd of 31,684 for a game at the Rose Bowl in Pasadena, California. The following month, the team played before 50,041 in Rio de Janeiro, Brazil. The team was doing so well, in fact, that they split into two units. The second unit, headed by Babe Pressley, drew a total of 500,000 fans on a 41-game trip through South America while the first team, featuring Tatum and Haynes, rambled for the second straight year through a packed-house tour of Western Europe and North Africa.

The team's tour of Europe came at a time of rising anti-American feelings on the Continent. Cold-war tensions between the United States and its chief Communist adversary, the Soviet Union, threatened to embroil Europe in another catastrophic conflict. And on the Korean Peninsula, an American-led coalition of United Nations forces was engaged in a bloody "police action" against North Korea and its powerful ally, the People's Republic of China. While the Globetrotters were experiencing the sting of anti-American sentiment during their stay in Paris, in Berlin, Sugar Ray Robinson, a legendary black boxer from Harlem, was dodging soda bottles and stones thrown by angry spectators after one of his bouts. A high-ranking U.S. government official stationed in Berlin, sensing that anti-American sentiment was threatening to boil over, requested that the Globetrotters come and play in an exhibition to help cool things down. Saperstein, wary of the Berlin mob that greeted the team at the airport, said, "At first I thought they were coming to get us when I saw this

*Abe Saperstein (right) points to a map that shows the sites and dates of games between the Globetrotters and a team of collegiate All-Americans. The tour proved immensely popular.*

big mob rush our bus. But then I realized they just wanted to shake our hands."

The official who had set up the game estimated to Saperstein that no more than 10,000 people would show up. On game day 75,000 people crammed the Berlin stadium. The Globetrotters heard their share of cheers from the enormous crowd, but it was Jesse Owens who stole the show. Owens had dominated the 1936 Olympics in Berlin, winning gold medals in the 100- and 200-meter dashes, the long jump, and the 400-meter relay. But the German leader Adolf Hitler had refused to congratulate Owens, who, as an African American, had shattered Hitler's myth of a superior "Aryan race." Fifteen years later, at halftime of the Globetrotter game, Owens returned to the stadium in Berlin.

"I've never seen anything like it, before or since," said Marques Haynes. "They must have given him an ovation for at least 45 minutes." Saperstein added, "I thought the Germans were going to tear the joint apart. It was the darnedest thing I ever saw in a quarter century in this business. I almost cried, I felt so good."

After the Berlin game, the U.S. State Department sent the Globetrotters an official letter of thanks, the gist of which would become the cornerstone of the Globetrotters' identity for years to come. The letter, which extended an offer of help to the team on any future ventures, included the line, "The Globetrotters have proven themselves ambassadors extraordinary of good will wherever they have gone."

With the State Department now on their side and with rave reviews and fan acclaim greeting them seemingly anywhere they went, the Globetrotters decided it was time to have done with it and finally circle the globe, see it all, go absolutely, positively everywhere. In 1952, to celebrate the 25th anniversary of his barnstorming team, Saperstein threw together an around-the-world tour that started in Recife, Brazil, in late April and ended just over five months later in Honolulu, Hawaii. In all, the Globetrotters would traverse 52,000 miles, visit 34 nations (approximately 6 nations a month), and play games in opera houses, baseball parks, soccer stadiums, airplane hangars, blood-spattered bullrings, malodorous fish markets, a drained swimming pool or two for old times' sake, and even an occasional basketball arena. Along for the ride were not only Saperstein, Tatum, Haynes, young J. C. Gipson, old Babe Pressley, one-armed Boyd Buie, and the rest of the Globetrotter players, but also jugglers, singers, dancers, a Belgian unicyclist, an Albanian fire-eater, a husband-and-wife trampoline team, a pair of table tennis pros, an accordian player named Tony Lavelli who doubled as a Globetrotter stooge, and a seven-ton, 150-section hardwood floor. The latter was for the several places along the tour that had no basketball court for the simple reason that basketball, up to the time the Globetrotters arrived, had never been played in that particular neck of the woods.

In Amsterdam, the Netherlands, the Globetrotters played though it was only 33 degrees. In Taipei, Formosa, they played in 120-degree heat, wearing water-soaked turbans to keep themselves cool. In Athens, Greece, it was so hot that the team waited until 10 P.M. to take the court, but even so, the temperature still topped 100 degrees and the asphalt court they played on melted, trapping their sneakers in the sticky goo. The court was then hosed down, making it too slippery to play on, so a chemical was used to dry it, which was okay until a torrential downpour hit. The Trotters experienced more rain in Nancy, France, but played on, Goose Tatum taking the court in a colorfully striped, antique, full-body bathing suit and Haynes putting on his usual dribbling display with just his right hand while he held an umbrella with his left. In Kuala Lumpur, Malaysia, the team had to rectify a promoter's overbooking by playing a doubleheader in 120-degree heat, with the second game ending in a tropical monsoon. In Egypt, the players donned scarves to protect themselves while they played through a sandstorm.

Through it all the Globetrotters kept playing their game to rave reviews. Even the pope chimed in with words of wonder. At the Roman Catholic leader's summer palace in Castel Gandolfo, Abe Saperstein asked, "Would Your Holiness like to see a small demonstration?" Pope Pius XII replied in the affirmative, and Bill Brown, Babe Pressley, Leon Hillard, Clarence Wilson, and Josh Grider, dressed in suits, whipped up an impromptu Magic Circle act as Saperstein snapped his fingers and led the team in whistling "Sweet Georgia Brown," the team's theme song.   Beneath flowing robes, a holy foot could be seen tapping along to the tune.  "These young men are certainly very clever," said the pope before calling for an encore.  "If I had not seen it with my own eyes," he concluded, "I would not have believed it could be done."

The team's biggest problem on the tour was the disappearing Goose.  It was not a new problem.  A couple of years earlier, as the team rode a train bound for Seattle from St. Louis, Tatum had stepped off, without any baggage, in Omaha, Nebraska, disappearing from sight for a week.  Another time, as the team was passing through Gary, Indiana, Tatum had the bus driver stop so he could go into a drugstore by the side of the road.  Somehow, he vanished again.  Six days later, after the team had played their way through Michigan, Ohio, and Pennsylvania, they walked into a locker room in White Plains, New York, to find Tatum awaiting them, ready once again to play.  During a visit to Rome, Italy, Goose fell out of sight, resurfacing many days later in jail in Dallas, Texas, for having punched a cop.

"That man is a contradiction," said Abe Saperstein of his star.  Leon Hillard agreed: "It was amazing.  You'd see Goose out on the floor, laughing and playing tricks, but as soon as he was inside the clubhouse, he just turned it off, like an electric switch. He was like two people."

Marques Haynes, who saw what Hillard saw and also saw Tatum do things like give the headwaiter at a restaurant a $50 tip one night and the next night in the same restaurant toss his uneaten meal disgustedly at the headwaiter's feet, said of his enigmatic teammate, "Dr. Jekyll and Mr. Hyde had nothing on Goose."

During the around-the-world tour, Goose disappeared in Algiers.  He later explained that he want-

ed to see the Casbah, the city's famous native quarter. "I had heard so much about it, I just wanted to see what it was like. So I took off." After going a week without Tatum, Saperstein went into the Casbah to search for him. After looking for a day and finding nothing, Saperstein, still wandering the streets at 4 o'clock in the morning, heard a horse and buggy pull up behind him and a familiar voice say, "Hey boss! Get on board. I'll give you a free ride." He turned. It was Goose.

Life on the road was difficult and wore Tatum down. Despite the Globetrotters' enormous success in the early 1950s—besides the round-the-world tour, the team had also starred in two Hollywood movies, Go, Man, Go and The Harlem Globetrotters—the players still had a tough row to hoe. During their long barnstorming season in the States, they struggled from place to place in an old Army

*The Globetrotters demonstrate the Magic Circle, their famous pregame warm-up ritual conducted to the strains of "Sweet Georgia Brown," before a game played in an outdoor stadium in Rome, Italy.*

carryall bus so cold in wintertime that icicles formed on the ceiling. "We had to keep them broken off so they didn't stick in our heads if we hit a bump," said Haynes. Worse, the Globetrotters, despite their newfound world renown, were still second-class citizens in many places they traveled to in America. Haynes recalled, "We could eat only by sending one of the players through the back door of the restaurant to ask for sandwiches to go. Worse was at gas stations. We had to go 300 miles just to find a men's room that allowed colored people. We used to have to go into hotels with insect spray. We'd take the covers off and spray our mattresses, underneath and on top, to kill the bedbugs."

Haynes began to feel he deserved a bigger share of the team's revenue. "Mr. Saperstein wouldn't cut the players into the two movies we made, the appearances we did, and other fringe earnings," he said. Sweetwater Clifton added, "Abe just didn't want to pay any of us any money. I can't understand that. He could have kept the whole team going and still made his money and everybody would have been happy." Even Clifton, however, would come to see that Saperstein held nearly all the cards, and that options were limited for black basketball players. Though Clifton made it to the NBA, an enormous number of black players did not immediately follow him. Many believed that the league maintained quotas, trying to keep no more than one black player per team. After his NBA career ended, Clifton would eventually wind up back on Saperstein's payroll.

Marques Haynes ended his dealings with Saperstein in 1953. "If you can't agree with a man financially, you can't play with him," he said. But the flight of the World's Greatest Dribbler from the Harlem Globetrotters entailed more than just a disagreement over finances. During one of their final, ultimately fruitless contract talks, Saperstein leaned toward Haynes and uttered, "Negroes don't need as much money as the white man."

Haynes had a chance to play in the NBA but decided instead to strike out on his own. He started a barnstorming team called the Harlem Magicians. The team prospered for many years, proving that a black man could not only be the star of the show in basketball, but that he could run the show, too.

# 6

## "That Genuine Laugh"

IN THE SPRING of 1952, Abe Saperstein received a letter from a Wilmington, North Carolina, teenager that began, "My ambition is to become a Globetrotter." Something in the letter caught Saperstein's attention, though he had never heard of the young man who wrote it. Maybe Saperstein saw something of himself in the youthful player, who, with every word in the letter, seemed to say that he would simply refuse to take no for an answer. "I have the spirit and go-getiveness it takes to become a Globetrotter," concluded the 18-year-old, whose name was Meadow George Lemon.

Saperstein asked Marques Haynes, who was at that time still with the Globetrotters, to look Lemon over when the team played a game in Raleigh, North Carolina. Haynes did more than just look him over. Just as the game was about to begin, he took Meadow Lemon into the locker room and tossed him a Globetrotter jersey.

"Suit up," said Haynes. Lemon could barely find words to speak. Haynes explained that he would not have time after the game to give Lemon a try-out, so the youth would have to show his stuff during the game. The ambitious youngster was suddenly so nervous he could barely lace up his sneak-

*Globetrotters Joe Buckhalter (top) and Clarence Wilson pose for a photograph to publicize an October 1960 engagement in Chicago, Illinois. Despite its famous affiliation with Harlem, Chicago was the team's original hometown.*

ers. It was almost too much for him to believe—he was about to step onto the court as a Globetrotter.

Lemon had been in love with the team since he was 11 years old. At the movies one day he had seen a short newsreel feature on the Globetrotters. Lemon had been hooked from the moment the music of "Sweet Georgia Brown" had started. By the time the feature was over, Lemon's life had been forever changed. As he wrote in his 1987 autobiography, "The athletic ability was fantastic, of course, but there was something else. It was the joy, the teamwork, the sense of family. It was the most wonderful thing I had ever seen in my life. I stared, not blinking, hardly breathing. In a flash, I knew I wanted to be on that team, the Harlem Globetrotters."

Throughout his adolescence, Lemon had kept that dream alive, working ceaselessly on his basketball game, a game that did not come easy for the sometimes awkward youngster. A kind of hunger fueled his dedication to the dream. For Meadow Lemon, the Globetrotters became a dream of wholeness, something to believe in in the face of the tough realities of his life.

Lemon was a lonely boy in a fractured family. His mother lived far away (in Harlem) and his father, a notorious gambler, chose to let aunts and uncles raise his son. Thinking about the Globetrotters whipping the ball around in the Magic Circle, everyone laughing, slapping palms, and hollering, Lemon said, "I wanted that feeling of family and teamwork that I never really had. I'd never seen a Globetrotter in person but something drew me to them as if they would finally be my first real home and family."

After overcoming the panic that seized him in the locker room in Raleigh, Lemon went out and seized his golden opportunity. After the game, an impressed Haynes promised to tell Saperstein that Lemon could play. Lemon then got the blessing of

his idol. "You're a good-lookin' ballplayer, Lemon," Goose Tatum said.

Like Tatum, Lemon's career with the Globetrotters was delayed by a stint in the armed services. As Tatum had done before him, Lemon used the years in the service to polish his game while playing for his army base's team in Germany. Inspired by Haynes's recommendation, Saperstein himself went out of his way to take a look at Lemon while the Globetrotters were on a European tour. "The day you get your Army discharge," Saperstein told Meadow Lemon after watching him play, "you've got yourself a job."

While Lemon was on the brink of seeing his longtime dream of becoming a Globetrotter come true, Goose Tatum's career with the team was turning into a nightmare. All the years he had spent on the road seemed to be taking their toll. Tatum

*Seen here on arrival at Wembley Airport in London, England, for a Globetrotters game in May 1959, Meadowlark Lemon succeeded Goose Tatum as the team's center and lead clown.*

Goose Tatum signs the bond agreement after posting bail following his arrest for income tax evasion in Dallas, Texas, in January 1961. Perhaps the most beloved player in Globetrotters history, Tatum might also have been one of the most troubled.

explained his weary malaise by saying, simply, "I been around too much." His sudden disappearances from the team were becoming more frequent than ever. He dropped out of sight for 17 games, his longest absence yet. "I don't know what the hell happened to the guy," said an exasperated Saperstein. "It's the damnedest thing I ever saw." Saperstein tried to grab his melancholy star's attention by suspending him for 30 days without pay. That only served as the final volley in a relationship between the two men that had reached a breaking point.

By 1955 Marques Haynes had his team, the Harlem Magicians, up and running. Tatum bid Saperstein farewell and joined his old Globetrotter teammate on the Magicians. Though he would help the Magicians become a successful operation, the departure from the Globetrotters marked, for Tatum, something of a farewell to the mass-public adulation he had received as a member of Saperstein's team. As he drifted farther from the limelight, Tatum's personal demons seemed more and more to get the better of him. His many scrapes with the law climaxed in 1959 with his imprisonment for 90 days for failure to pay back taxes. In the years that followed—which would be the final few years of his life—he struggled increasingly with financial woes and failing health.

Saperstein would be hard-pressed to replace the on-court genius of Goose Tatum. The man could simply do things no one else could do. Jesse Owens, who knew something about being a cut above other men and who had watched Tatum extensively while serving as the Globetrotters' traveling secretary, said, "You know why Goose has no peers in the world today? Because he's a great tonic for people in these unsettled times. People are always looking for some way to forget their cares. Goose provides something—that genuine laugh which strikes deep within you and leaves a warm glow."

There never could be another Goose Tatum. But the possibility that someone else could come along with the rare ability to draw out, as Owens put it, "that genuine laugh," was recognized by no less an expert than Tatum himself. Before he left the Globetrotters, he made a point of taking Meadow Lemon aside after his tryout in Raleigh. "A couple times watchin' you," Tatum told the newcomer, "I thought I was looking in a mirror, no kiddin'. I thought, 'Here I am on the bench, and there I am on the floor.'"

Saperstein also knew he had a potentially great performer on his hands in Lemon. Although he could not play straight basketball as well as the players on the earlier Trotter unit that beat George

Mikan and the Lakers, he seemed from the beginning to have some of the same laughter-coaxing charisma that Tatum had. It was also clear from early on that Lemon would work with a passion and determination that bordered on obsession in order to become a great entertainer. After games, Lemon would stay behind in his hotel room to practice his moves in front of a mirror as his teammates went out to a bar or a nightclub. "I don't know how many room windows I broke all over the country before I perfected my skills with a basketball," he once said.

By the end of his rookie season in 1955, Lemon had earned a new nickname—"Meadowlark," pinned on him by teammate Josh Grider—and a trial run as head clown of the Harlem Globetrotters. Tatum had quit, Sam Wheeler, Tatum's first replacement, had broken his knee, and Bob "Showboat" Hall, Wheeler's replacement, had come down with pneumonia. Saperstein gave Lemon a chance to be the lead clown for a game in Chicago. Thinking of the opening minutes of that game, Lemon recalled, "From somewhere deep inside me came a joy and even a voice that I can only use while I'm on the court in the heat of a game."

Meadowlark Lemon came alive as he never had before, whipping passes from the pivot to his cutting teammates, laughing, beaming, pulling reems, yakking nonstop in a high-pitched voice that reached to the very last row of the arena, dancing with the referee, slapping hands with fans in the front row, tossing in his clumsy-looking hook and then bowing with mock pomposity as if the whole world had been saved from sure ruin by the shot, then smiling a smile that rippled out to everyone in the building like warmth from the sun. "I was making people happy," Meadowlark said. "I felt the capacity crowd having fun because of me. But no one," he added, "was having a better time than I was."

Though he would not give Lemon the full-time lead clown job for another year, Saperstein knew by this time that the Globetrotter clown of the future was Meadowlark Lemon. This knowledge must have eased Saperstein's mind a bit, but he remained troubled by the recent loss of Marques Haynes and Goose Tatum. For the first time in a decade, the team was without the type of star attraction that packed people into the stands on the strength of his name alone. To rectify this situation, Saperstein set his sights on signing an All-American basketball player from the University of San Francisco named Bill Russell.

Saperstein watched and waited as Russell powered his college team to 55 straight wins and back-to-back NCAA championships. After Russell had added a gold medal with the U.S. basketball team in the 1956 Olympics, Saperstein made his ill-fated

*Abe Saperstein introduces the Globetrotters' newest player, Wilt Chamberlain, to the press on June 18, 1958. The Globetrotters agreed to pay $65,000 for a season's play, which was then a record salary for a basketball player.*

*Meadowlark Lemon flips up an underhand shot while falling to the makeshift basketball floor pieced together in the track-and-field stadium in Helsinki, Finland, for the Globetrotters' game there in May 1961. The team's globetrotting ways brought them to games played in virtually every conceivable kind of setting.*

attempt to lure the young player to the Globetrotters. He reportedly offered Russell $50,000 just for signing his name to a Globetrotter contract, a staggering figure considering the fact that even the highest-paid NBA stars did not receive that much in an entire year. It later came to light that the offer was closer to $15,000, but what turned Russell away from the Globetrotters was not what Saperstein offered but the way he offered it. When Russell and his college coach, Phil Woolpert, met with Saperstein, the portly impresario reserved all talk about

business for Woolpert while treating Russell like a child.

"All Saperstein said was hello and goodbye to me," Russell said. "He just talked to Woolpert, telling him what the Globetrotters could do for me and how much money I could make. He never said a word to me, treating me like an idiot who couldn't understand what the conversation was about." By the end of the meeting, Russell had resolved never to play for Abe Saperstein. "If I'm not smart enough to talk to," Russell would write in his autobiography, *Go up for Glory*, "then I'm too smart to play for him."

Whether it ever occurred to him or not, Saperstein was falling more and more out of tune with a rapidly changing world. Late in 1955, a resounding early shot had been fired in the African-American civil rights struggle when Rosa Parks, a seamstress from Montgomery, Alabama, defied the entrenched Jim Crow laws by refusing to give up her bus seat to a white passenger. Many black men and women all over the country were, after years of silent suffering, refusing to be treated as anything less than dignified human beings. Russell shunned the Globetrotters, in short, because Saperstein did not treat him like a man.

It is unlikely that the fiercely competitive Russell, who would go on to lead the Boston Celtics to 11 NBA titles in 13 seasons, would have lasted long as a Globetrotter anyway. As more and more black players opted to compete in the NBA, the Globetrotters could no longer be counted among the top teams in the world. It marked a turning point in the history of the team. The Globetrotters became, more than ever, first and foremost an entertainment act.

The perfect man to lead the team into their new era took over the lead clown job for good at a Globetrotter game at Yankee Stadium in New York

City at the end of the 1957–58 season. Saperstein, said Meadowlark Lemon, "was giving me my final test for lead clown by putting me before the biggest crowd that would ever see me play." Almost from the moment Lemon stepped onto the portable floor laid down across the stadium grass, he had the crowd of 65,000 on his side. "My smile always gets to an audience, and it did that day." Even with the biggest of crowds, even in a cavernous stadium where the fans were far from the basketball court, Lemon had a way of inviting every last person watching into the very heart of the rollicking show. Laughter cascaded down from the stands, and Lemon fed off that laughter, diving ever more completely into his role as a clown, and the laughter doubled, and Lemon fed off it some more, and the laughter doubled again.

Saperstein made Lemon the lead clown of the Globetrotters for the coming 1958–59 season. Lemon would hold that job for over 20 years, showing, in literally thousands of games all over the world, his gift for bringing crowds alive. "My smile was the door opener," Lemon said. The door swung open and the laughter flowed in. "I couldn't believe the applause, the laughter. It was almost physical, lifting me, inspiring me, warming me. I couldn't get enough of it. Every night I could hardly wait to charge from the locker room into the gym to get another fix of crowd reaction."

The 1958–59 season was a big year for the team, and not just because it was Lemon's first year as head clown. Saperstein, two years after failing to sign Bill Russell, signed a college star who made Russell's fame seem slight in comparison. A 20-year-old, 7-foot colossus named Wilt Chamberlain, bored with dominating the competition in the college ranks, left the University of Kansas after his junior year and joined the Harlem Globetrotters. Abe Saperstein had his star attraction.

In the years that followed, Chamberlain would go on to the NBA and perform incredible, record-shattering feats of near-mythic proportions, such as scoring 100 points in a single game, or averaging 50 points a game for a season, or smashing the league rebounding mark for a game by corraling 55 boards against none other than his nemesis, Bill Russell. But for the 1958–59 season, Chamberlain was the consummate Harlem Globetrotter. Having joined the team in part, as he said, "because they had a great tradition," Chamberlain came to embody many of the things that made that tradition great.

Like the Globetrotters of the past, Chamberlain was an outstanding all-around athlete. To highlight

*Hoops in the Holy City: The Globetrotters dribble their way across Rome, Italy, in July 1963. While there, the Trotters even demonstrated their roundball repertoire for the pontiff, Pope Paul VI.*

his abilities, Saperstein brought him away from his accustomed position near the basket, effectively making Chamberlain into a point guard. Many of the fans who swarmed to the Globetrotter games that year expected to see a turgid, earth-bound behemoth. Instead, they were presented with the stunning specter of the lithe and agile giant, decked out in Globetrotter red, white, and blue, dribbling past defenders at the top of the key, passing to his teammates for easy scores, or else gliding toward the basket for a graceful lay-in, a trademark finger roll, or an arena-rocking skyscraper slam.

Besides the desire to become part of the Globetrotter tradition, Chamberlain also wanted to be a Globetrotter for the simple reason that the team "just seemed like a lot of fun." Chamberlain shared with the lead clown, Lemon, a strong impulse to please people when he stepped onto a basketball court. In this regard he differed greatly from Bill Russell, whom, after leaving the Trotters, he would battle at the pinnacle of the basketball world for a decade. The dour warrior in Celtic green once stated, "I can honestly say I have never worked to be liked."

Boston sportswriter Bob Ryan recognized that Chamberlain was Russell's opposite in this regard. Ryan said of Chamberlain, "What he wanted more than anything else was to be your friend." A Globetrotter, or any kind of entertainer, could only be spurred on to crowd-pleasing greatness by such a desire.

Chamberlain quickly became an integral part of the Globetrotters' traveling bazaar of wonder. Unlike many of the Trotters, who, like Goose Tatum, had long ago wearied of the never-ending road, Chamberlain reveled in the chance to explore the world. He would come to regard his time with the Trotters as a great learning experience and as the most fun-filled year of his life. In later years, as

Chamberlain endured an increasingly pressure-filled and joyless career in the NBA, Saperstein said of him, "We didn't put pressure on him. We played a fun game. He didn't get his teeth knocked out. The NBA is no fun for Wilt." Chamberlain often agreed with Saperstein's assessment.

Not long after Chamberlain left for the NBA, another player with equally astonishing skills joined the Globetrotters. But the playground legend named Connie Hawkins would never look back with a smile on his years with the team. Much as Chamberlain's ebullient experiences revealed many of the finest aspects of the team, Hawkins's travails demonstrated what seemed to him to be the dark side of life as a Harlem Globetrotter.

Hawkins came to the Globetrotters because he had nowhere else to go. Implicated (falsely, it was proven years later) in a gambling scandal, Hawkins had been dropped by the University of Iowa basketball program and subsequently banned by the NBA. There was no question that Hawkins was good enough to play in the pros. "Connie Hawkins plays against us in the summer," said Knicks all-star center Willis Reed at the time. "We all know he'd be a superstar in the NBA." Hawkins briefly showcased his high-flying skills in Saperstein's shabbily thrown-together American Basketball League. When the league collapsed, Hawkins had few options. Basketball, the game in which he showed himself to be nothing less than an improvisational genius, was the only thing he knew. Saperstein offered Hawkins a job, and he took it.

A shy and introverted young man, Hawkins was still suffering the aftereffects of a childhood spent in extreme poverty in the Bedford-Stuyvesant section of Brooklyn. Among other things, Hawkins had endured the scornful laughter of the other kids in his neighborhood, who taunted him for his ragged, ill-fitting clothes. "I'd felt like a fool so much in my life," said Hawkins, "I didn't want to make more situations where people laughed at me." In other words, Hawkins did not want to play the clown. This reluctance to ham it up for the fans, as well as the fact that he felt his skills eroding as he played all his basketball against second-rate competition, soon turned Hawkins against the Globetrotters. He could not define the reason for his bitterness until years later. Looking back, he said, "What we were doing out there was acting like Uncle Toms. Grinnin' and smilin' and dancin' around—that's the way they told us to act, and that's the way a lot of white people like to think we really are."

Race relations had advanced since the Globetrotters' earliest days. Black basketball stars like Bill Russell and Oscar Robertson, if born a few years earlier, may very well have had to go against their impulses as, to use Nelson George's words, "no-nonsense brothers" and adorn their fierce games with gags and clowning. Now they could simply play the type of game they were born to play. But the fact remained, as Hawkins said, that many white people, whether they realized it or not, still clung to and wanted to perpetuate the safe image of the black man as a clown.

Hawkins saw a little deeper into the racism permeating American society the first time he traveled with the Globetrotters to Europe. "As soon as I got off the plane," he said. "I felt like this pressure came off me. People treat you different here. Man, they smile at you. Back home I always felt people were down on me cause I'm colored." In Europe, Hawkins was told by his teammate Tex Harrison, "Ol' dude, enjoy it over here. On this side of the ocean—maybe 'cause we're Trotters—we're kings. Back home, we're still nothing."

Hawkins came to resent the man who signed his paychecks. The resentment stemmed in part from the fact that the paychecks seemed so small; even

after a couple of years with the team, Hawkins was making the equivalent of $35 a game. The total amount he earned in his four years as a Trotter added up to about what Chamberlain made in a month for the Philadelphia Warriors of the NBA. But an even larger reason for Hawkins's resentment derived from Saperstein's patronizing attitude toward his players. "As long as you played the role of the grateful boy," Hawkins said, "Abe was good to you. You had to let him know you thought he was great, that he was always right. You had to go along

*Charles "Tex" Harrison of the Globetrotters tries a left-handed lay-up against the Baltimore Rockets in March 1960. A veteran Trotter, Harrison tried to take the sensitive young superstar Connie Hawkins under his wing, but Hawkins never became enamored of the Globetrotter way of life.*

with all his hangups and stereotypes."

Even Saperstein's top employee, Meadowlark Lemon, had his problems with the boss man. "On the one hand," said Lemon, "he was the guy who made my dream come true. On the other hand, I felt I had to treat him as a father figure, a Santa Claus, to get anything out of him. I had to be subservient and beg and plead to get a break." But Lemon believed that there would be no Harlem Globetrotters without Saperstein, not only because of his skills as a promoter, a public relations genius, a businessman, a motivator, and even something of a visionary, but also because, as Lemon said, "he hired blacks when it was unfashionable."

On May 15, 1966, as he prepared for a game in Charlotte, North Carolina, Meadowlark Lemon heard the news that Abe Saperstein, who had been in poor health for several months, had suffered a fatal heart attack. The enigmatic founder of the Harlem Globetrotters was dead. "My mouth went dry," Lemon said. "The boys cried. I had to force myself to be funny. I did it only because Abe would have wanted the show to go on."

Lemon's tribute struck to the heart of the enigma that was Abe Saperstein. He was a man who had, above and beyond his many failings, devoted his life to putting on one of the greatest shows on earth. His close friend Tony Lavelli had summed up Saperstein a few years earlier, saying, "The Globetrotters are his life."

Harry Saperstein tells a story of his older brother's final days that shows the truth of Lavelli's words. "Abe wanted to see that game down in Long Beach," Harry began, "for whatever reason I don't know. But I picked him up and took him and his wife Sylvia down to Long Beach. Now he was so weak that I almost had to carry him. He wouldn't use crutches but I had to get underneath his shoulder and almost half-carry him into the stadium.

"But once the Trotters came out on the floor it was just like he was reborn again. It was amazing— he was not that sick man at all, he was very wild. I don't think anyone laughed any harder at Long Beach Stadium than Abe did."

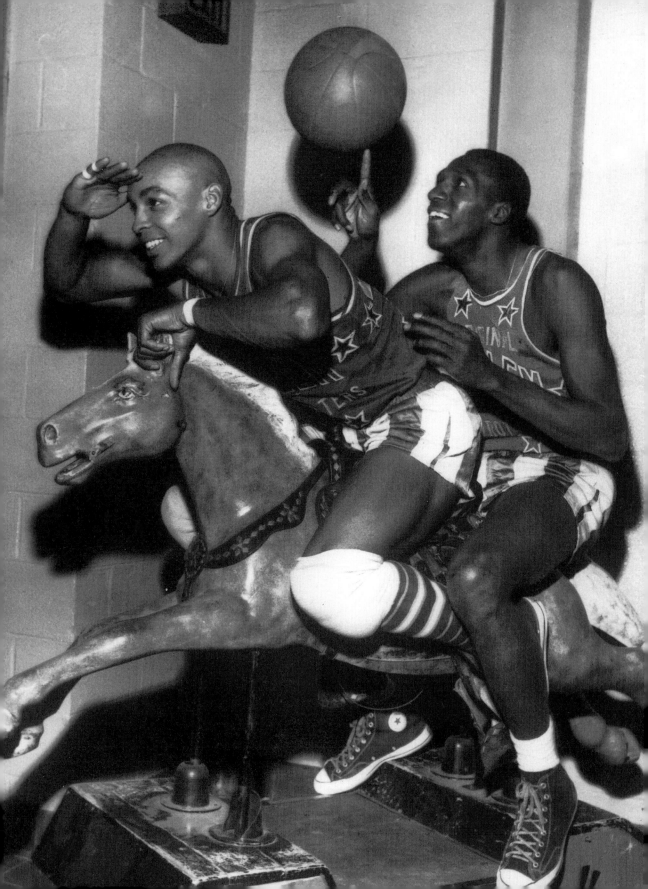

# 7

## "Miracle Men"

**A** LITTLE OVER a year after Abe Saperstein's death, the Harlem Globetrotters were sold for $3,710,000. The Globetrotters had grown from six guys eating bologna sandwiches in the cramped confines of a Model T Ford to a multimillion-dollar business. Saperstein, of course, deserves much credit for that. He also deserves credit for looking out for many of his ex-players. Meadowlark Lemon observed, "Several of his long-time players were given other jobs in the organization when their playing days ended." Inman Jackson, for example, who had been with Saperstein from the second season of the Globetrotters, still had a job with the team at the time of Saperstein's death.

But not all the Globetrotters were taken along for the ride, and lost in the shower of accolades for Saperstein was the fact that the greatest sacrifices were made along the way by the black players. While Saperstein continually pumped life into the show, it was the players, with their stunning skills and flair for entertainment, that made up the very heart of the Harlem Globetrotters.

Throughout the many years of their existence, no one represented more of the essence of the Globetrotters' greatness than Goose Tatum. Tatum,

*The incredible skill of Frederic "Curly" Neal (front), who has been called one of the greatest shooters ever, became the perfect foil for the clowning of Meadowlark Lemon (rear). Curly's charismatic personality made him a favorite of the fans, especially children.*

who had been in and out of hospitals with a liver ailment, fell deathly ill at his home in Dallas, Texas, on the morning of January 18, 1967. He died at a hospital later that day at the age of 45. Marques Haynes heard of the death on his car radio and traveled, along with his wife and old Globetrotter teammate Josh Grider, to the announced site of Tatum's funeral, Fort Bliss, Texas. When they got there, a grave digger at the cemetery told Haynes that Tatum had already been buried. No one had been there. "They didn't do nothin'," the grave digger said. "They drove up, backed the hearse up to the grave, lowered the casket and took off."

Haynes went to the grave and did what he could. He read from a Bible he bought at a drugstore for $2.98. "The Lord is my shepherd, I shall not want," Haynes began. It did not seem right, and Haynes could barely continue. No one had come to the funeral at all. "Goose was the greatest drawing card that had ever been," said Haynes. Then Haynes finished reading the prayer.

Just prior to his death, Goose Tatum had given some words of encouragement to a young Globetrotter who had caught his eye. "You're doing great, kid," Tatum said. "Keep up the good work, keep 'em laughing, and good luck." The young player, who was named Hubert "Geese" Ausbie, smiled back at the smiling Globetrotter legend. Ausbie would help his team "keep 'em laughing" all through the coming decade of the 1970s, as the famous barnstorming club grew bigger and better than ever. From Goose came Geese, and the Harlem Globetrotters' magic bus rolled on.

Ausbie embodied the excellent mix of basketball talent and entertainment flair that the team offered in the early 1970s. Before his professional career, Ausbie had starred at Philander Smith College. In his senior year he scored more points than any other college player in the nation save for two

*Curly Neal shows off his famous dribbling skills while Joe Dennis of the Washington Generals rushes to stop him.*

eventual Hall of Famers named Oscar Robertson and Elgin Baylor. But Ausbie's talent as a clown eclipsed his considerable basketball skills. Even before he joined the Globetrotters, people could see that Geese Ausbie was put on this earth to be funny. "Ausbie was a naturally humorous man," said Connie Hawkins. "He was lovable and lackadaisical and he always had a smile."

Inman Jackson, who had seen all the great basketball entertainers come and go, took one look at Ausbie and hastened to the owner of the team. "You've got to take this boy," he told Abe Saperstein. "He is a born clown."

Saperstein signed Ausbie and also made one more great addition to his beloved team. "He brought in a young man named Curly," said Meadowlark Lemon, recalling one of Saperstein's final moves. "It was no longer just me out there. It became Curly and me, me and Curly."

Frederic Douglas "Curly" Neal quickly became Meadowlark Lemon's perfect sidekick. As Marques Haynes had earlier complemented Goose Tatum, Neal now did the same for Lemon by showing off his brilliant dribbling prowess and astoundingly accurate long-range shooting. Nat "Feets" Broudy, a longtime NBA executive, compared Neal favorably to an extensive list of Hall of Famers, saying, "I've seen all the greats—Paul Arizin, Jerry West, Bill Sharman, Pete Maravich, Sam Jones . . . but Neal was fabulous. Without a doubt, he's one of the greatest shooters I've seen."

Neal's overwhelming appeal derived from more than just his ability to dribble and shoot. First of all, his nickname-earning clean-shaven head, a rare look for the time, made him stand out in any crowd.

*The Washington Generals traveled with the Globetrotters and played against them in exhibition games. They beat the Globetrotters only once.*

But more than that, Curly Neal always exuded an ebullient and highly contagious feeling of easy joy. Fans, especially children, were drawn to the beaming, bald-headed star like slivers of metal to a magnet. Neal attributed his success, and the success of the team, to a rare kind of generosity of spirit. "I guess that's what made the Globetrotters over all the years," Neal said, smiling, seeing how simple it all could be: "We just give." No one embodied this generosity of spirit more than Curly Neal.

Besides Neal, Ausbie, and Lemon, the team also gave their fans talented former college stars like dribbling expert Pablo Robertson, who had won an NCAA championship in 1963 with Loyola University, and Dave "Big Daddy" Lattin, who had starred for Texas Western's NCAA titleholder three years later. They gave their fans a playground legend named Jumping Jackie Jackson. "He had this shot called 'The Double Dooberry With a Cherry on Top,'" recalled Connie Hawkins. Jackson, Hawkins explained, took off at the foul line and pump-faked twice in midflight before slamming the ball down through the rim. "Nobody in the world could do that shot but him. People went crazy every time he did it."

Jackson and the other new stars played alongside old hoopsters such as Bob "Showboat" Hall, who had been plying his trade since the late 1940s. Another old-timer, big J. C. Gipson, a Globetrotter since the team's first world tour, showed the younger players that being a Globetrotter often took a lot of hard work, sacrifice, and pure determination. "I saw J. C. get out of a sickbed to play," Connie Hawkins said.

Gipson was not the only Globetrotter to play through pain. "Meadow'll have a splitting headache," reported muttonchopped teammate Nate Branch, "and he won't let Doc near him with an aspirin, but he hears that announcer say, 'Globetrotters' and he pulls his head up and goes two hours as if nothing is bothering him." Lemon played, night in and night out, no matter what. He completely dwarfed Randy Smith's NBA-best streak of 906 games by starring in more than 7,500 consecutive Harlem Globetrotter games.

And Lemon gave it his all, night in and night out, no matter where. "Lemon gets involved 100%," said Tex Harrison. "He doesn't care if there are 5,000 or 50,000 in the stands. He believes he can be great at anything, and he'll do whatever he must to convince you." Lemon's pursuit of excellence as an entertainer did not allow him to sit out a game, even if he had good reason. "I was from the old school where if you sprained your ankle, you just laced your sneaker up tighter and hobbled around until the pain passed," he said.

Lemon, named player-coach of the team in 1971, soon found that his old-school ways often put him at odds with the younger players. "I thought my ballplayers were babies," Lemon bluntly admitted. The ballplayers, in turn, saw Lemon as something of a tyrant. From early in his career, Lemon had always strived to be the center of the show. He saw that fans made a lot of noise when everything ran through him, and he was determined to make that happen every game. "On the court Meadowlark has to control everything," Tex Harrison said. "Look, he is the show." This need for control frequently put him at odds with anyone who threatened to steal the spotlight. He fought with Connie Hawkins and before that, even tried to take on Wilt Chamberlain. "One time Lem dove at Wilt's throat," said Harrison. "Dipper just caught him in the air. He lifted Meadowlark over his head and held him there until he calmed down."

In the early 1970s, the squabbling between Lemon and the other players intensified. Like Saperstein before him, Lemon had a very clear idea

of what the Globetrotters were. He knew they were entertainers, pure and simple, and for continued success, they had to perform like entertainers. "We're only playing for pride out there," he said. "We got no pennant to push us. Some of the fellows don't understand either that this is family-type entertainment. We're playing to please. I'll say, 'Why did you shoot?' They'll say, 'I was open,' and they don't understand that it may be no good for the show even if they make it."

The demands of the show began to wear on many of the players. In 1971, they went on strike, leaving Lemon, whom they saw as part of management, behind to be not only the center of the show but the whole show, period. It was a tactical mistake, as management correctly surmised that Lemon was the one man they could not afford to lose. A leader of the strike, Frank Stephens, after

*The Harlem Globetrotters walk a picket line in their 1971 strike against team management. The players' demand that they be "treated as men and given [their] human dignity" created controversy among critics who questioned whether the nightly clowning was turning team members into "Uncle Toms," a racist stereotype that depicted blacks as undignified, obsequious, and overeager to please whites.*

*Lou Dunbar (left), Curly Neal (right), and the rest of the Globetrotters joined the popular 1960s television characters Gilligan (third from left) and the Skipper (second from left) in the feature-length film* The Harlem Globetrotters on Gilligan's Island. *The film, unfortunately, was a critical flop.*

outlining demands for a pension plan, a better insurance plan, more meal money, and "decent salaries," said, "We want to be treated as men and given our human dignity."

Critics of the Harlem Globetrotters took Stephens's statement and ran with it. The question of whether or not the players were stripped of their dignity on a nightly basis was raised. Were they forced to be Uncle Toms? Lemon answered the critics by saying, "Look, if I'm Tomming by making people laugh, then all comedians, white or black, are Uncle Toms."

Another player, John Smith, whose father was the chairman of the Arizona Civil Rights Commission, also refuted the criticism. He asked, "How can you Uncle Tom when you're making money?"

The strike died within three weeks, the players

surrendering most of their demands when they learned that Lemon was recruiting replacement players. Frank Deford described fan reaction to the strike in *Sports Illustrated.* "To the public," he wrote, "it was as if Santa Claus' elves had gone out." But when the team came back, all was forgiven, at least with the Globetrotters' growing legion of young fans.

The Globetrotters' continuing success with kids was attributable to a feeling, as Deford had implied, that the players were mythic, magical characters. Marie Linehan, Saperstein's longtime personal secretary, saw the phenomenon develop from very early on. "I think what it is with the Globetrotters," she explained, "is that the kids have to believe in something, and they don't believe in Santa Claus anymore. The Globetrotters give them the myth with reality. They win every game, so they are miracle men, which means the kids don't have to make a decision about them. And the kids know what's going to happen in every game, they know the whole scenario. But you see, this doesn't disturb them. On the contrary, it makes the kids more a part of it."

The Globetrotters did win just about every game they played in. Midway through the 1970–71 season, they had won 2,495 straight contests, a streak that dated back to 1962, covering eight undefeated seasons. During the streak, the closest the Washington Generals, the team that traveled with the Globetrotters, came to toppling their perpetual conquerors was a two-point loss in Long Island in the late 1960s. The Generals had a chance to tie with seconds left, and they got the ball into the hands of their founder, coach, and designated long-range set-shot hurler, Louis "Red" Klotz. Klotz, his travel-worn face brightening with beautiful, ageless, eternal hope, hoisted one of his antediluvian specialties. It rolled around the rim and out. Game over.

Klotz had tasted victory decades before, albeit as a nondescript benchwarmer for the 1947–48 title-winning Baltimore Bullets, a team that the usually celebratory writers for the *Sports Encyclopedia: Pro Basketball* dubbed "A Dull and Nameless Champion." In the Bullets' less-than-glorious play-off climb, Klotz had played sparingly, scoring exactly a point a game. Not long after that, Klotz was out of the big leagues and running a team that played the Globetrotters in exhibitions. "Jackie Gleason has Art Carney. Abbot has Costello," said Klotz, naming two of the great comedy teams of the 20th century. "And the Globetrotters got us.

"We've lost thousands of games," Klotz continued, "give or take a few hundred either way." Despite this record, which might have made lesser men want to hide in a dark room for the rest of their days on earth, Klotz remained upbeat. In fact, in the midst of their eight-year losing streak, Klotz remained downright defiant. "It is going to happen one of these days," he vowed. "We are going to beat the Harlem Globetrotters again. You can count on it."

Many people thought that the Generals could never win for the simple reason that they were not supposed to. Klotz bristled at this claim. Far into the dark heart of his colossal losing streak, he said, "Neither Abe Saperstein, who was a very close friend of mine, nor the Globetrotters' new ownership, ever told me to lose a game. And I've never told my players to lose." Still, lose they did, again and again, until the mere thought of a Washington Generals victory seemed as far-fetched as the idea that someday Hershey's Chocolate Kisses will suddenly start raining from the sky.

Then, on January 5, 1971, in Martin, Tennessee, the unthinkable happened. The Washington Generals beat the Harlem Globetrotters. After his team's valiant win, a befuddled Red Klotz said,

"You'd think the crowd would have applauded us. Instead they hissed us as we walked off the court."

Klotz, who still runs the Generals today, his team winless since that night in Tennessee (the current losing streak is approaching 9,000 games), knew as well as anyone that his team was merely the foil for the true heroes of the show. In the early 1970s, the Globetrotters had an unbreakable hold on the hearts of their biggest fans. One of their young fans from that time, highly reputed 1970s pop-culture trivialist Pete Millerman, recalls, "In my mind, there was nothing the Harlem Globetrotters couldn't do. They were superhuman. They were larger than life."

The Globetrotters had been all around the world several times. But they went even farther still

*Meadowlark Lemon exhibits his trademark antics and has some fun with a referee at Madison Square Garden during a 1973 game.*

in this triumphant era by voyaging into the magical, Technicolor, childhood never-never land of Saturday-morning cartoons. Hanna-Barbera, the cartoon company that brought forth to the world, among other things, Magilla Gorilla, Yogi Bear, Dastardly and Muttly and Augie Doggie, now sparked to life a cartoon version of the Harlem Globetrotters.

Kids all over America, giddy from wolfing sugar-choked bowls of King Vitamin or Count Chocula or Alpha-Bits, watched Meadowlark lead his animated cohorts in and out of hilarious (and utterly preposterous) situations. In one show, the old lady who drove the team bus, a purely fictional character known simply as "Granny," got taken hostage in the Himalayas by a kingdom of hulking snow monsters. The Globetrotter players themselves, plus their mascot—a white, mule-faced, sneaker-wearing dog named Dribbles—soon joined Granny in captivity but gained their freedom by besting a team of the abominable snowmen in a basketball game. In another show, the team was imprisoned by a mad scientist named Professor Creeply, who desired to gain fame and riches by creating a dominant basketball team of eight-foot-tall robots. The Globetrotters again, after battling with Creeply's vicious pet alligators, busted out of the villain's clutches by virtue of their incomparable basketball skills, beating the robots soundly (final score, for the record: 248-6).

Back in the real world, Marques Haynes rejoined the team after nearly 20 years away. He showed he still had all his old ballhandling magic, improvising his nightly dribbling act like a jazzman blowing out a soulful solo. Meadowlark Lemon was moved to proclaim, "Marques is the best, as old as he is, the best in the business." Haynes had a similar awe-inspiring effect on his teammates off the court. When Globetrotter Nate Branch was asked to describe Haynes, he said simply, "A great man."

Although Haynes was too late to join Meadowlark, Geese, Curly, B. J., Gip, Pablo, Dribbles, and Granny in cartoonland, he did get a starring role in a Saturday-morning live-action kids' show called *The Harlem Globetrotters Popcorn Machine*. This show, conducted by a hip little Afro-headed kid named Rodney Allen Rippy, featured the team in gags, spoofs, skits, and ballhandling wizardry, plus some assorted shenanigans, a fair dose of monkey business, and a generous sprinkling of inspired tomfoolery.

The Harlem Globetrotters were everywhere. Besides the cartoon and the live-action show, they had starred in a feature-length movie called *The Harlem Globetrotters on Gilligan's Island*. (One reviewer, after calling the film "inane gibberish," recommended that "Chinese water torture would be preferable" to watching it.) The Globetrotters also had their own comic book, and many of their games were televised on *ABC's Wide World of Sports*. They also appeared in a growing number of television commercials for assorted products. Advertisers clamored to draw on the well-known and highly favorable image of the Globetrotters. The Coca-Cola Company banked on the team's joyous style in one commercial, which featured Curly happily swigging soda as voices sang, "Have a Coke and a smile!" In another ad, a voice-over intoned an airline's slogan—"Getting people together"—as the Globetrotters whipped a ball around the inside of a 747 jet airliner.

The team in the star-spangled uniforms had become an American institution. On December 6, 1974, the Globetrotters went to the White House to receive a presidential citation from Gerald Ford. President Ford thanked the team for giving millions of fans, as he put it, "much more than basketball, but also the priceless gifts of love and laughter."

# 8

## Doing It Right

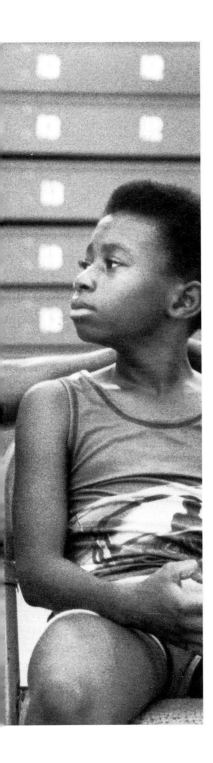

FOR THE HARLEM Globetrotters, giving "the priceless gifts of love and laughter" was never easy, not even after the early days of segregated hotels, blizzards, and crowded sheep shacks had passed into memory. Despite the resounding success the team enjoyed in the 1970s, certain hardships persisted for the players, the painful cost of a life spent on the road. "It never gets any easier," said Nate Branch. "The last time I left home, my little boy grabbed me at the airport and said, 'Don't go, Daddy.' You know what that does to you? I heard him crying and calling all the way to the gate."

The uncompromising toll of constant travel hit Meadowlark Lemon the hardest of all. His frequent absence from home contributed to the gradual disintegration of his marriage. The bitter divorce then received a gruesome punctuation mark when Lemon's ex-wife stabbed him in the back with a six-inch steak knife. Ever the unflagging entertainer,

*Meadowlark Lemon left the Globetrotters in 1978 and went on to a variety of projects, including the film* The Fish That Saved Pittsburgh. *A still from the film shows Lemon as the Reverend Grady Jackson discussing an upcoming basketball game with ball boy Tyrone Millman (played by James Bond III).*

Lemon shrugged off the knife wound and boarded a plane to London for a game.

Unfortunately for Lemon and for his millions of fans, it was beginning to appear that a divorce between the Harlem Globetrotters and their long-time star also loomed on the horizon. A contract dispute turned Lemon and the team management against each other, and certain festering problems, such as longtime petty jealousies, turned Lemon and his teammates into enemies. Lemon could sense that he was being pushed aside. He played out the string in the 1977–78 season, and then quit the team that had been his whole life since he was 11 years old.

He remained in the public eye, starring with hoop legend and avatar of cool Julius "Dr. J" Erving in a cinematic basketball fairy tale called *The Fish That Saved Pittsburgh*. He also scored a part in a sit-uation comedy starring Maclean Stevenson titled *Hello, Larry*. In the show, Meadowlark Lemon played his best role—Meadowlark Lemon— but, alas, *Hello, Larry* soon followed Rodney Allen Rippy and the dog named Dribbles into pop-culture oblivion, never to be heard from again.

Lemon started his own barnstorming team but quickly found the going rough. One problem was that, in many ways, his heart remained with the Harlem Globetrotters. "I love the Globetrotters," he wrote in his 1987 autobiography. "I always have. I always will. Frankly, nothing would make me hap-pier than to somehow be hooked up with the Trot-ters again someday."

In 1978, the role of Harlem Globetrotters lead clown passed from Meadowlark Lemon to Geese Ausbie. "Some men shoot for the moon," Ausbie said. "Some try to get a corner on the money mar-ket. But I've never had any ambitions along those lines. When I was seven years old, I saw the Harlem Globetrotters play, and they made such an impres-

sion on me that I made up my mind that I wanted to be a great basketball player with them, and to make people laugh, like they do."

Geese gave voice to a sentiment that was shared by many of his teammates on the Globetrotters. For them, taking the court and entertaining fans as they traveled the world amounted to a labor of love. "I've satisfied my childhood dream," Ausbie concluded. "How many people can say that? I'm 'doing my thing.' When the fans laugh, I feel like I'm ten feet tall. It's a wonderful feeling."

Unfortunately for Geese and the rest of the team, in the mid-1980s the team's popularity, which had been climbing for 30 solid years, finally showed signs of slowing. The NBA, which had struggled in

*In 1985, in an effort to re-kindle the team's energy, the Globetrotters went coed. Lynette Woodard, the first woman to join the team, infused the Globetrotters with a new burst of enthusiasm and caused a surge in fan support. Here ABC sports commentator Cheryl Miller (left) interviews Woodard (right) and teammate Jackie White.*

*In 1993, businessman Mannie Jackson (below) bought the flagging Harlem Globetrotters and put his efforts into revitalizing the team. Himself a former Globetrotter, Jackson recognizes that the Globetrotters are more than just entertainment, emphasizing both the team's importance in sports history and the integral role that community service plays in the team's identity.*

the 1970s, now experienced a surge in attendance and fan interest as superstars such as Magic Johnson, Larry Bird, Julius Erving, and Michael Jordan captured the imagination of basketball fans everywhere. The high-flying, inventive, and often spectacular NBA game of the mid-1980s, which had been pioneered by the Globetrotter teams of old, seemed, ironically, to draw fans away from the Globetrotters. Also, the team itself had begun to lose that vital spark. "The comedy," said Globetrotter team president Earl Duryea, "had become frayed and stale."

In an attempt to revitalize the team and to renew fan interest, the Globetrotters decided, just

before the start of the 1985–86 season, to stage a special tryout. Duryea and new coach Russell Ellington invited 18 of the best women's basketball players to fight it out for a spot on the team. Critics of the idea, some Globetrotter players among them, suspected that the whole scheme was a publicity stunt that would ultimately compromise the skill level of the team. The criticism began to fade as the women proved early on in the tryouts that they could play some serious ball. "After the trials began," said Duryea, "it was no longer a question of can a girl play, but which one?"

Among the 18 former college stars, one woman rose to the top. At the end of the tryouts, 25-year-old Lynette Woodard, who had starred at the University of Kansas before captaining the U.S. women's basketball team to a gold medal in the 1984 Olympics, listened as her name was announced as the first female Harlem Globetrotter. "The joy that I felt was unbelievable," she recalled of that moment.

It should have been no surprise to Woodard that she won the job. After all, the Globetrotters were in her blood. She had first been introduced to the team as a little girl when her cousin, none other than Geese Ausbie, showed her some of the tricks of the trade. "It was unreal," she said. "I couldn't believe the things he was doing with a basketball." Although the young Woodard tried to imitate Ausbie's magic—breaking up the house in the process— she did not start to think about joining the team until years later. Despite the fact that there had never been a woman competing against men in professional basketball, let alone a woman on the Globetrotters, she began to dream about wearing the Globetrotter uniform as a junior in college. When the dream came true and Woodard joined the team, she practically burst with happiness. "I got the chance of a century," she said. "It's the first time in history it's been done. Since the earth was created, let alone when basketball began. I'm in basketball heaven. How sweet it is! How sweet it is!"

Woodard's overflowing enthusiasm pumped new life into the team. For many of the longtime Globetrotters, it had become increasingly difficult to enter into the mirthful spirit of the act, night in and night out, all season long. Things changed when Woodard arrived. "She comes to play," said 10-year veteran James "Twiggy" Sanders, "and she comes to have fun. And I'm not going to let her have more fun than I'm having."

The team experienced an upsurge in fan support after welcoming Woodard aboard. But only a few years later, the Globetrotters ran into a problem that threatened the team's very existence. The company that owned the team, the International Broadcasting Corporation, went into bankruptcy in 1991. The team's tour schedule got sliced in half and attendence dropped 67 percent in 1991 and 1992. At that point Mannie Jackson, a brilliant, high-ranking executive at a Fortune 100 company called Honeywell, Inc., saw a business opportunity that he could not pass up.

In June 1993, Jackson, who had actually played with the team in the 1960s, headed a partnership that bought the Harlem Globetrotters. For the first time ever, the Harlem Globetrotters were owned by a black man.

Like many of the men who had kept the Globetrotters alive throughout the years, Mannie Jackson had worked his way up from humble beginnings. Born in a boxcar in Illmo, Missouri, at the tail end of the Great Depression, from a young age he set his sights on getting a college education. After moving to Edwardsville, Illinois, Jackson began to exhibit the basketball prowess that would earn him the Illinois "Prep Player of the Year" award as a senior in high school. He went on to star for the University of Illinois, and then took a crack at the NBA. At that time, however, because of an unwritten agreement between team owners, the door was not fully open for black players to enter the NBA. Only the absolute best black players earned spots on NBA teams. So Jackson took his excellent passing and shooting skills to the Harlem Globetrotters.

The young player, who never seemed to miss a chance to learn something new or improve himself in any way possible, grew from the experience of being a Globetrotter. "At an early age," Jackson said, "it allowed me to use basketball as a means of bringing smiles to thousands of fans as I gained unique insights into people and cultures around the world."

Jackson had mostly positive memories of playing with the team. But the savvy executive would never allow a decision of such magnitude to be swayed one way or another by nostalgia. Above all, it was a business decision, and Jackson went after it with the same tenacity, vision, and calm levelheadedness that had landed him the job at Honeywell as senior vice president in charge of a $2.3 billion division. These qualities had also brought him recognition in the *Journal of Business Strategy* for being one of the nation's top 50 corporate strategists and in *Black Enterprise* magazine for being one of the nation's 40 most powerful and influential black corporate executives. Jackson saw in the Harlem Globetrotters a business with a high potential for growth.

The Globetrotters' new leader quickly took control of the team. According to one of Jackson's colleagues in the Executive Leadership Council, a social network for black executives, Jackson had the sort of powerful charisma that makes a leader. "In a room that starts out with 30 conversations," said Alvaro Martins, "there will be a lot fewer after he arrives and a big group around him." Jackson also showed right from the start the ability to make all

*After almost 70 years, the Harlem Globetrotters are still going strong. Here, players Lou Dunbar, Matthew Jackson, and Osborne Lockhart (left to right) show General Colin Powell a few tricks.*

those in the team's organization, from scouts to players to office secretaries, feel like they were going to be a part of a Harlem Globetrotter renaissance. Martins noted, "He makes people feel they are a piece of the puzzle that makes things work."

Jackson came up with several innovations to revamp the Globetrotter act, including the addition of high-energy rock music and a team mascot named Globie. At the same time that he was looking to the future with these changes, the former player was attempting to shine a powerful light on the team's past. He drummed up Hollywood backing for a forthcoming movie about the Globetrotter struggle for recognition and acceptance during the late 1920s and 1930s. He also set up a "Harlem Globetrotter Legends Award" to salute some of the players who had carried the team to greatness over the years. Curly Neal, Connie Hawkins, Geese

Ausbie, and Bob Karstens—the oldest living Globe-trotter—all received the award during the 1993–94 season.  Said Jackson, "These players were among the pioneers of the sport who brought the level of play up to where it is today."

One of the great African-American basketball pioneers, Sweetwater Clifton, passed away around the time that Jackson was taking the reigns of the Globetrotters.  Clifton had worked as a cabdriver in his hometown of Chicago in the decades following his basketball career.  Before he died he cast a wistful look back to the days when he circled the globe, playing hoops as he went.  "I been all over the world," he said.  "I been to France, Hong Kong, Singapore, Manila, Australia, been to Italy, Belgium, Holland, Switzerland, Germany, been to South America, Rio, Lima, Buenos Aires, even Cuba.  We was there before they put the Iron Curtain up.  I've had a great life.  I can't complain.  The only complaint I got is I would like to have just one year made big dollars, you understand?"

At the peak of his career, as he was sold from the Globetrotters to the New York Knicks, Clifton had been bilked out of several thousand dollars by Abe Saperstein.  Clifton would come to blame himself for the incident, saying, "If you're not up on things you just have to bounce the way the ball bounces."

Mannie Jackson did not want to profit from any ignorance on the part of his players.  He wanted to make sure that his players were, as Clifton had put it, "up on things."  Jackson outlined his vision of a more well-rounded, business-savvy Globetrotter player, saying, "I want a team of players who are comfortable with kids or giving presentations in boardrooms."

The new owner of the Globetrotters, as a former player, would never make the mistake of overlooking the importance of the players, both past and present. "The games played on the court today," said

Jackson, "are like musical compositions with different notes originating from the masters—Globetrotter greats like Goose Tatum, Geese Ausbie, and Meadowlark Lemon, and current standouts like 'Sweet Lou' Dunbar, Matthew 'Showbiz' Jackson, and Barry 'High Rise' Hardy."

Jackson retooled the Globetrotters' preseason training camp to include classes for the players on African-American history and media relations. The players came to see more clearly that they were more than just entertainers. As Darryl Dawkins, the 6-foot 11-inch backboard-shattering ex-NBA star, extraterrestrial philosopher, and mirthful poet, who joined the Globetrotters for the 1994–95 season, explained, "Being a Globetrotter is a way of life. There's a lot of responsibility that comes with wearing the famous red, white, and blue uniform and it's more than just playing great basketball, it's also about being a good person."

The Globetrotters maintain their tradition of extensive charity work by giving aid to the United Negro College Fund and to the United Way's "Success by Six" program. "It's a humanitarian mission," said Jackson of the charity work, "and that's always been part of the Globetrotter identity. It's one of the most profound things we do as an institution.

"The Harlem Globetrotters are one of America's greatest assets," Jackson continued. "Because they are so much a part of sports history, I feel a major responsibility to make it happen right. When I do things, I always ask, What would it look like done right?"

The Harlem Globetrotters seem to be doing it right. In Jackson's first year as owner, the team's total revenues doubled. Prospects for the future appear even brighter. "A lot of guys said the team would fold before March 1," Abe Saperstein was fond of saying, thinking back to the team's first year in 1927, "but they forgot to say what year."

As the team nears its 70th anniversary in 1997, it shows no signs of slowing down at all.  All-time Globetrotter great Curly Neal was asked how long he saw the team enduring.  He thought for a moment.  Then, as a smile spread slowly and easily across his face, he replied, "Just as long as the ball continues to be round."

1900  Abraham Saperstein born in London, England

1921  Reece Tatum born, May 3, in Eldorado, Arkansas

1925  Marques Oreole Haynes born in Sand Springs, Oklahoma

1926  Former Wendell Phillips High School players begin playing games in Chicago's Savoy Ballroom as the Savoy Big Five

1927  Ex-Savoy Big Five players and Saperstein form Harlem Globetrotters; team plays first game in Hinckley, Illinois

1928  Inman Jackson joins the Globetrotters

1934  Meadow George Lemon born in Wilmington, North Carolina

1939  Globetrotters place third in first World Tournament; Mannie Jackson born, May 4, in Illmo, Missouri

1940  Globetrotters win World Tournament

1942  Goose Tatum joins the Globetrotters

1946  Marques Haynes joins the Globetrotters

1948  Globetrotters beat Minneapolis Lakers in Chicago Stadium

1950  Globetrotters begin an annual series with a team of college all-stars; take their first trip to Western Europe and North Africa; Sweetwater Clifton, along with Chuck Cooper and Earl Lloyd, breaks the NBA color line

1951  Globetrotters play to a crowd of 75,000 in Berlin

1952  Globetrotters embark on a 34-nation around-the-world tour

1953  Marques Haynes quits Globetrotters to start his own team

1955  Goose Tatum leaves the Globetrotters; Meadowlark Lemon joins the team

1958  Wilt Chamberlain, after forgoing his senior year at the University of Kansas, joins the Globetrotters for a season

1960  Globetrotters travel behind the iron curtain to play a series of games in Moscow

1966  Abe Saperstein dies on May 15

1967  Goose Tatum dies on January 18

1971  Meadowlark Lemon named player-coach of Globetrotters

# CHRONOLOGY

1974    Globetrotters receive presidential citation

1978    Globetrotters compile their best record ever, 512-0; Meadowlark Lemon named in nationwide poll as fourth most popular personality in America, behind John Wayne, Alan Alda, and Bob Hope; Meadowlark Lemon stabbed by ex-wife; Meadowlark Lemon quits team to pursue career in Hollywood

1985    Lynette Woodard joins Globetrotters, becoming first woman ever to compete in professional basketball against men

1993    Mannie Jackson heads partnership to buy Harlem Globetrotters

Chamberlain, Wilton Norman, with David Shaw. *Wilt: Just Like Any Other 7-Foot Millionaire Who Lives Next Door.* New York: MacMillan, 1973.

George, Nelson. *Elevating the Game: The History and Aesthetics of Black Men in Basketball.* New York: Simon and Schuster, 1991.

Gibson, Bob, with Lonnie Wheeler. *Stranger to the Grime.* New York: Viking, 1994.

Lazenby, Roland. *The Lakers: A Basketball Journey.* New York: St. Martins Press, 1993.

Lemon, Meadowlark, with Jerry B. Jenkins. *Meadowlark.* Nashville: Nelson Publishers, 1987.

Peterson, Robert W. *Cages to Jump Shots.* New York: Oxford University Press, 1990.

Pluto, Terry. *Tall Titles.* New York: Simon and Schuster, 1992.

Russell, Bill, with William McSweeny. *Go up for Glory.* New York: Coward-McCann, 1966.

Salzberg, Charles. *From Set Shot to Slam Dunk.* New York: E. P. Dutton, 1987.

Vecsey, George. *Harlem Globetrotters.* New York: Scholastic Book Services, 1973.

Zinkoff, Dave. *Around the World with the Harlem Globetrotters.* Philadelphia: Macrae Smith Company, 1953.

# INDEX

# INDEX

# PICTURE CREDITS

JOSH WILKER has a degree in creative writing and literature from Johnson State College. He is the author of several Chelsea House volumes, including *Julius Erving* in the BLACK AMERICANS OF ACHIEVEMENT series, *A. J. Foyt* in the RACE CAR LEGENDS series, and *The Lenape Indians* in the JUNIOR LIBRARY OF AMERICAN INDIANS series.